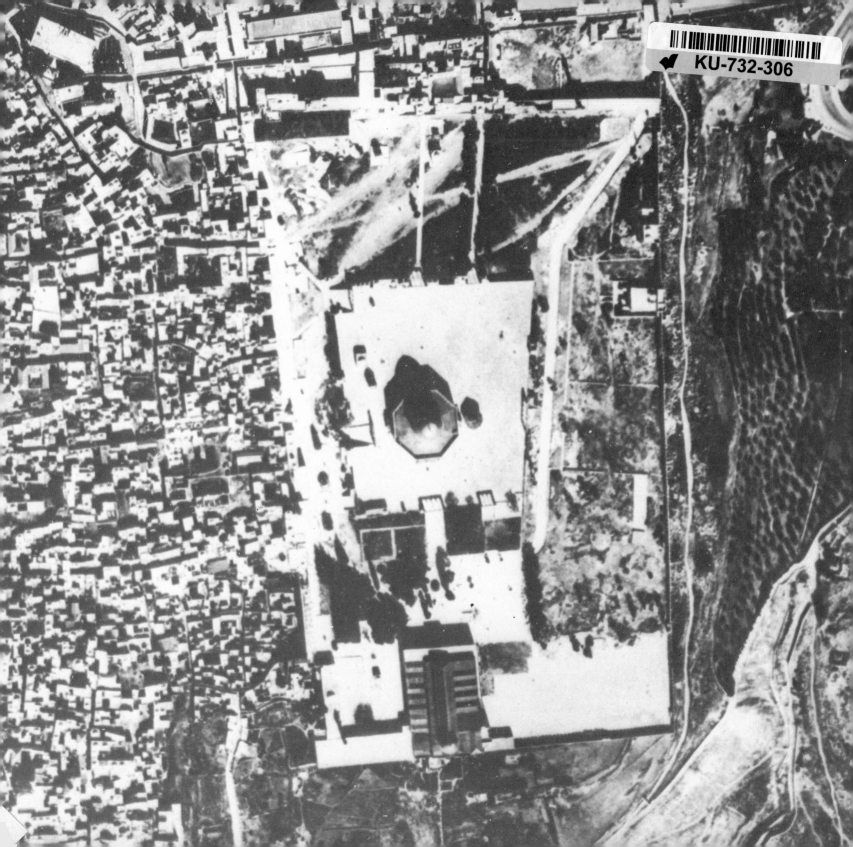

To dear Margaret

with many thanks
for innumerable kindnesses
both professional + personal —

May God bless you.

Your devoted friend

+Mario.

March 1977.

The Noble Heritage

Jerusalem and Christianity:
A portrait of the Church of the Resurrection

by
Alistair Duncan

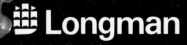
Longman

LONGMAN GROUP LIMITED.
LONDON

Associated companies, branches and representatives throughout the world

© Photographs: Middle East Archive (Alistair Duncan) 1974
© Text: Alistair Duncan 1974

First published 1974

ISBN 0 582 78039 X

Set in Monophoto Univers

Printed in Great Britain by Jarrold and Sons Ltd, Norwich

ACKNOWLEDGEMENTS
Acknowledgements and thanks are due to:
George Rainbird Ltd. for permission to reproduce the map from *Jerusalem* by Colin
Thubron (Heinemann).
Weidenfeld and Nicolson for permission to reproduce the quotation from *Israel and
the Holy Places of Christendom* by Walter Zander.
Stewart Perowne and Hodder and Stoughton for permission to quote the note on
the Holy Orthodox Eastern Church from *In Jerusalem and Bethlehem* (*Pilgrim's
Companion*) by Stewart Perowne.
The Y.M.C.A. of the Old City of Jerusalem for permission to photograph the bread-
mould from the collection of Dr Tewfiq Canaan (Jacket).
Fr. Aug. Spijkerman, O.Fr., for permission to photograph exhibits from the Museum
of the Convent of the Flagellation.
Professor Kenneth J. Conant for permission to reproduce sketches from his
monograph *The Original Buildings at the Holy Sepulchre in Jerusalem* (Speculum).

The author also gratefully acknowledges help given to him by the Greek and
Armenian Patriarchates in Jerusalem, the Franciscan Custodian of the Holy Land,
H. E. Cardinal Pio Larghi the Apostolic Delegate, Canon Edward Every of St
George's Cathedral, Stewart Perowne, and Father Charles Coüasnon O.P., together
with many other friends who contributed so much assistance.

*Right: the sixth-century mosaic map of Palestine
in Madaba (Jordan). This section shows
Jerusalem with the Church of the Resurrection
with its triple entrance below the
Cardo Maximus.*

Title page: The Unction Stone.

*End papers: an aerial photograph of the Old City of
Jerusalem, by courtesy of the Ministry of Defence.*

This book is dedicated to
the memory of
FLAVIUS VALERIUS CONSTANTINUS
Emperor of Rome, who
founded and constructed
the first Church of
Worship upon the site of
Christ's Passion and
Resurrection

It is also dedicated to
those who have lived,
worshipped, fought and
died in Jerusalem; in
sorrow, doubt,
persecution and joy;
steadfast and triumphant,
in the name of God

The Church of the Holy Sepulchre

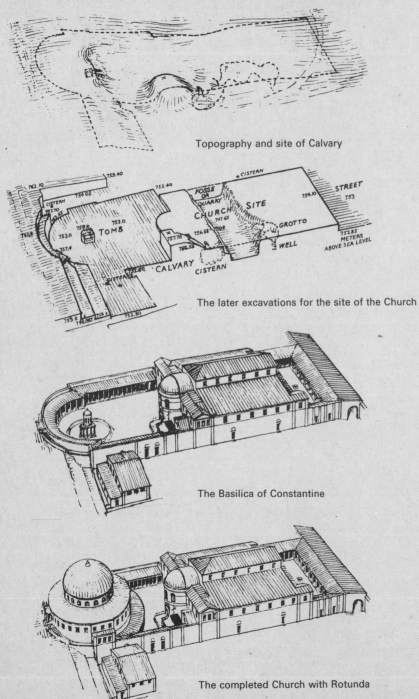

Topography and site of Calvary

The later excavations for the site of the Church

The Basilica of Constantine

The completed Church with Rotunda

1 Chapel of St James (Eastern Orthodox)
2 Chapel of St John (Eastern Orthodox)
3 Chapel of Forty Martyrs (belfry) (Eastern Orthodox)
4 Cisterns of St Helena
5 Convent of Holy Abraham (Eastern Orthodox)
6 Chapel of St John (Armenian)
7 Chapel of St Michael (Eastern Orthodox)
8 Chapel of Our Lady of Sorrows (Latin)
9 Grave of d'Aubigny
10 Moslem diwan and South Transept Entrance
11 Stone of Anointing (Armenian)
12 Chapel of Adam (Eastern Orthodox)
13 Place of Tombs of Godfrey and Baldwin I
14 Chapel of the Invention (Finding) of the Cross
     (St Helena) (Latin)
15 Chapel of Insults (Eastern Orthodox)
16 Chapel of Parting of Raiment (Eastern Orthodox)
17 Chapel of St Longinus (Eastern Orthodox)
18 Coptic Monastery of Dier El-Sultan
19 Cistern beneath Coptic Deir El-Sultan
20 Prison of Christ (Eastern Orthodox)
21 Arches of the Virgin (North Transept)
22 Franciscan Sacristy
23 Chapel of St Mary of the Franciscans (Latin)
24 Altar of St Mary Magdalene (Latin)
25 'Centre of the World' (Eastern Orthodox)
26 Chapel of Angel (Armenian)
27 The Tomb of Christ (Armenian)
28 Coptic Oratory
29 Syrian Chapel
30 Contemporary Jewish Tombs

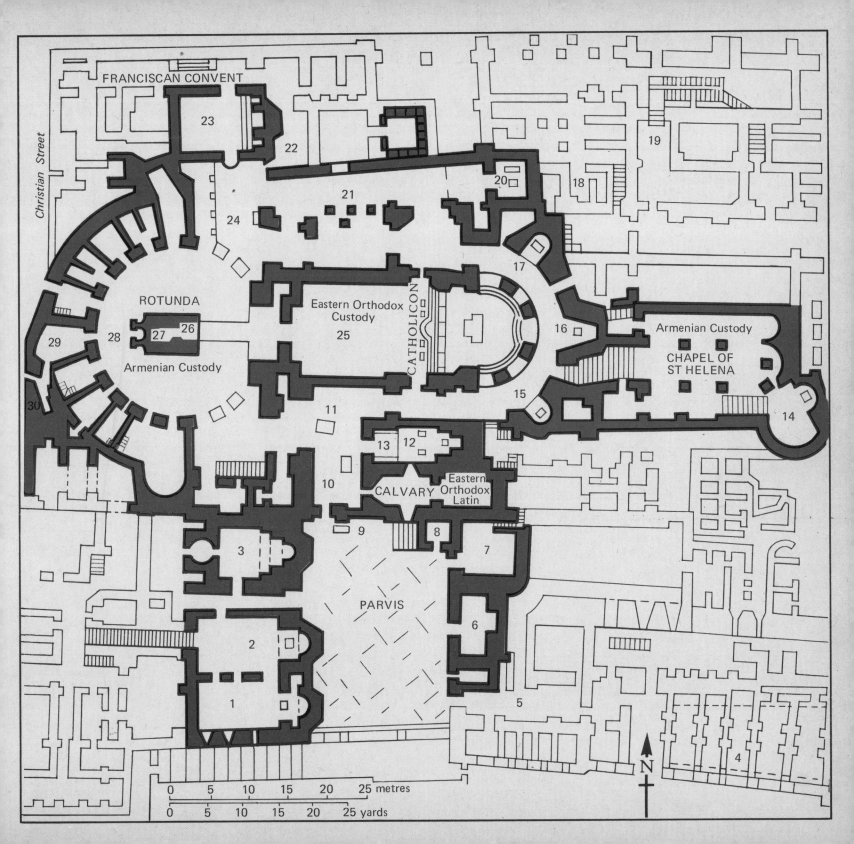

FRANCISCAN CONVENT

Christian Street

23

22

21

24

20

18

19

17

ROTUNDA

Eastern Orthodox
Custody

25

CATHOLICON

16

Armenian Custody

CHAPEL OF
ST HELENA

29

28

27 26

Armenian Custody

15

14

30

11

13 12

10

CALVARY

Eastern
Orthodox Latin

9

8

7

3

PARVIS

6

2

5

1

0 5 10 15 20 25 metres

0 5 10 15 20 25 yards

4

N

Preface

It is night. One solitary lighted window — witness of watchfulness, study or solitude — emphasizes the silence wrapped about the Old City of Jerusalem, huddled within its blanket of thick walls against the cold of the winter Advent's night. The hours are marked by chimes from the clock in the tower of the Franciscan Convent. With their passing, the bright stars grow faint, and the cloak of night slips from the shoulders of the sleeping city.

From beyond the Dead Sea and Moab, dawn approaches. The lightening sky is greeted by a peal of bells from the Church of the Resurrection, which is joined by *muezzins'* calls to prayer from minarets within the city. A sudden flurry and burst of song among the birds in the garden below give warning of the bustle of the day to come. Cocks crow, and the silver greys give way to chrome and blue as the sun now shimmers into sight beyond Mount Nebo. For a few minutes all is quiet again, as the ancient stones of the city warm to its rays. The day has safely dawned.

From my window, I look out across the roofs to the twin domes of the Church of the Resurrection. Fussed about and crowded by houses, monasteries, shops, mosques and chapels, it presents no clear outline or apparent individuality within the noisy city set around it. Symbolically, perhaps, this is as it should be, for the Church of Christ is for all humanity, and the redemption of mankind by God which He preached is essentially a matter of inward and spiritual grace.

Elsewhere, the congregational, as opposed to the memorial, churches, rise up in splendour and magnificence in order to enhance and further proclaim the faith that started in this turbulent city nearly two thousand years ago.

I do not propose to repeat in this book the background of history already set out in *The Noble Sanctuary*, the companion volume. Rather I try to depict within these pages an outline of Christianity in Jerusalem as seen through the history of the Church of the Resurrection; this ancient and hallowed building, which in itself is evidence of man's endeavour to glorify and demonstrate his belief in God.

May this small book serve to guide those who read it in their appreciation of this noble heritage, which has been handed down to them through many centuries of faith within the walls of Jerusalem.

Armenian patriarchal crown, originally an eleventh-century "Cap of Humility"; later encrusted with gold filigree, enamel and jewels.

Church of the Resurrection seen from the tower of the Lutheran Church of the Redeemer.

Introduction

The exact date, about A.D. 30–33, is uncertain, but this much is clear: the tomb was empty.

Beyond the small band of disciples and family, neither this, nor the event of Jesus' crucifixion, nor the drama of his trial — not even the brief years of his ministry — was of any recorded importance to the occupying power of Rome. Its faint ripple of effect was lost upon the troubled waters of political life in Syria Palestina at a time when rebellion was brewing beneath the surface of colonial rule. For many people, just one more self-appointed messiah had burnt himself out in a final act of torture and death; stretched out upon a wooden cross set up, as many others were, just outside the Gate of Ephraim, in what is now known as the "second" north wall of Jerusalem.

How Christianity spread and developed abroad is not the concern of this little book. That Christianity survived at all has been a matter for erudite explanation and analysis. In these pages we concern ourselves with that survival and development within the walls of Jerusalem. We may accept at once that it survived because it gave so much to so many people. To people oppressed, it offered freedom of the mind, and a recognition that material life would give way to life of the spirit, which was indestructible. Above all, it did away with the exclusiveness of God, bringing association and identification with Him within reach of the humblest person. Here for the first time was a man who so identified himself and all men with the marvel of created order, and with the direction of all natural and supernatural beings by a sublime and universal power, that he called that power his father. Here was one who stated quite categorically that God's Kingdom was not of this world; that it could not be judged by temporal standards, and that the dignity of the individual was of more importance than the ostentations and protocols of formal or collective presentation: that real life not only existed beyond the confines of the physical body, but remained dormant within it during its mortal span, to be recognized and admitted by anyone who chose. As well as this, he preached that man's actions and behaviour should be motivated by love — love for his fellow creatures and all things fine — and not by fear of the Law, with its emphasis on retribution and punishment from an exacting and unapproachable deity.

Yet faith, in its essential simplicity, is hard to project, and in his temples and places of worship man has endeavoured to construct forms and shapes that will enhance his aspirations and co-ordinate collective thought and purpose.

The Church of the Resurrection (or Holy Sepulchre) is indeed such a building; and recent restorations, long overdue, reveal once more the grace and power of its twelfth-century European architecture. But in the complexity of its chapels and areas appointed to the co-occupiers of its ancient site, it reveals much of the rivalries and dissensions which, once dominant, are now mercifully in retreat.

At a time of international perplexities and man's renewed uncertainties, it is proper to spend some moments upon the history of this building, which marks the focal point of a great religion; one whose basic message and exhortation even now exert most powerful influences upon mankind.

Seventh-century Greek cross of gold filigree containing fragments of the True Cross: later embellished with enamel insets and jewels.

A small fractured crucifix of the twelfth or thirteenth century, found near Jerusalem by Franciscan monks.

Calvary to Constantine (A.D. 30 to 324)

The small community, perhaps a few hundred strong, of Jesus' disciples and followers who continued to meet after his crucifixion were all Jews, living within and observing the structure of the Law. Their variations of its practices included amendments to fit into the philosophical pattern of the new fraternity. Pentecost, their harvest festival, was an occasion of natural excitement; of Canaanite or even earlier origins, it attracted large numbers of people to Jerusalem for its celebration. It can therefore be appreciated that at such a time, during a period of acute emotional tension and after the crucifixion of Jesus, communal prayer would stimulate such psychic phenomena and manifestations of the Holy Spirit as are described in the Acts of the Apostles, Chapter 2. In this book, there is space only to accept the fact of this first Christian Pentecost; and to recognize its supreme significance in the founding of the Church of Christ.

Before this day, those who believed in the teaching and the resurrection of the Nazarene carpenter's son were a small domestic community, banded together for self-support and mutual care at a time of increasing social and religious uncertainties, and of plots and upheavals that cannot be over-emphasized. From now on, the course of action was clear: the message of Christ's doctrine was to be taken and broadcast, to be received by whosoever willed.

Thus the apostles began to preach in Palestine to the heterogenous mixture of peoples who made up its population. This included Greeks and Romans from the military and civil services and from the commercial colonies set up along the coastal plain, as well as the indigenous Canaanites, Samaritans, and other tribal communities. But if the original call had seemed to be locally directed, it was now turned outwards towards all men.

In A.D. 49, although the centre of Christianity had moved away to Antioch, the First Council was held in Jerusalem under its Patriarch James. Persecution and discrimination, manifestations of intolerance by the Jewish authorities, finally brought about the complete separation of the new Christian communities at this time, and "pagan" converts were admitted.

Recruitment continued principally among the Gentiles, with small groups of Jewish Christians providing a number of schismatic sects. Finally, by the time of the siege and destruction of Jerusalem by Titus, son of the Emperor Vespasian, the Christian community took no part in the city's defence, having fled into Transjordan after the execution of James the son of Zebedee, one of the original twelve apostles, and after Paul's arrest by the Sanhedrin.

One member of the Sanhedrin, alone, appears to have counselled wisely. To his everlasting credit, the Rabbi Gamaliel, son of the priest Hillel, had earlier stated: "Men of Israel, take care what you do with these men . . . for if this plan or undertaking is of God you will not be able to overthrow them. You might even be found opposing God."

But, by rejecting this advice, and by driving the Christians out of Jerusalem, the Sanhedrin played a decisive part in ensuring that the new faith would be spread further abroad.

During the Passover of A.D. 66, the long-awaited revolt broke out. Led by an extremist organization, the Zealots, the campaign was directed not only against the Roman

Silver lamp and mosaic-covered arch on Latin Calvary.

Latin Chapel of Calvary. (Left: shrine of Our Lady of Sorrows.)

occupying power, but against all who showed signs of moderation or conciliation towards them. Countermeasures by the Romans exacerbated the situation by being inefficient and slow, allowing time for a Jewish administration to be set up which was even able to mint its own coins. As in all liberation movements, the "doves" were soon eliminated by the "hawks", and terror, matched by counter-terror, was inflicted upon the whole population, Jew and Gentile alike.

Now Rome herself, as opposed to local commanders, began her inexorable response. The Fifth, the Tenth and the Fifteenth Legions marched into Galilee and overwhelmed all resistance on their route south. In Jerusalem, the situation became totally self-destructive, with rival Jewish factions slaughtering one another ("Blood flowed from every corner of the Temple walls") and destroying one another's food stocks and provisions in their own struggle for local dominance. Titus Flavius Vespasian, who was later to become emperor, was in no hurry, and his troops leisurely prepared their initial assault. To his son Titus was left the task of occupying the Holy City, now reduced to a state of starving chaos by its own defenders.

In spite of the civil war which raged amongst them, they still, incredibly, maintained an effective defence against the legions, giving ground only after inflicting heavy casualties upon their attackers. Titus therefore decided to call off the attack, to seal off the city, and watch the inhabitants complete his task for him. But the witnessing of the atrocities and the onset of cannibalism obliged him to seek a swift end. In the final assault the Temple was burnt, by accident it is claimed, the city was destroyed, and the remaining population sold into slavery. Tacitus quotes the great Caledonian chieftain Calgacus as saying, "When the Romans make a wilderness, they call it peace." Even then, the Jewish people in Syria Palestina were not subdued. Nor were those in the Diaspora less acquiescent, and a general uprising throughout the eastern empire was savagely put down.

The Emperor Hadrian, who succeeded Trajan in A.D. 117, conducted an official visit to Syria in 130 and 131 and decided to build a new city upon the ruins of Jerusalem: Colonia Aelia Capitolina, named after his family. This, coupled with an imperial edict prohibiting the physical mutilation which was widespread in the Eastern Empire, and which included circumcision, further exacerbated the smouldering resentment of the Jews. From 133 to 135 a merciless guerilla war was fought. This time the Jews, under Simon Bar Kochba (or Kozeba), who claimed to be the Messiah, were united but avoided all direct combat. The lessons of the previous revolt had been learnt, and the Romans were obliged to regain control village by village, strongpoint by strongpoint. In the end, the country lay stricken and exhausted, and its people were sold into slavery. The new city of Aelia Capitolina rose up as a garrison town for the Tenth Legion. Within it, a statue of Hadrian stood on the site of the Holy of Holies. A temple of Venus covered the former place of imperial crucifixion and the place of Jesus' burial, beside the new forum, alongside other temples to Jupiter Capitolinus and Juno. Baths, a theatre, a hippodrome and a circus, all took their places in a typical transversal layout, which can still be discerned today. The walls were not built up, but formal monumental gateways were erected; the remains of the East Gate may still be seen in the Convent of the Sisters of Zion. Occasional columns, which formerly lined the two

Greek cross of John Palologus (1440) containing fragments of the True Cross. This side is diamond-studded.

The Eastern Orthodox Chapel of Calvary.

main streets — the north-south Cardo Maximus and the east-west Decumanus Maximus — are to be found in the city today. The town, of far less importance than the provincial capital, Caesarea, on the coast, slowly grew and expanded as traders, ancillary workmen, craftsmen and all the other civilian attachments to a military establishment settled under its aegis. But by decrees, neither Jews nor Christians of Jewish origin were allowed to live there. For a time the Hebrew Christians lived elsewhere in Syria Palestina, under cover, for whilst Judaism was accepted by Rome as a religion, Christianity was not, and although not initially banned, its adherents were required by edict to sacrifice to the gods of Rome, and failure to do so was severely punished. So the roll of Christian martyrs grew within Palestine.

It would appear that the first church building of the Gentile Christians, as opposed to informal meeting places, was on the western hill, now known as Mount Zion. Perhaps it was placed here in memory of the Last Supper and the places where the apostles had gathered. Be that as it may, it was certainly established by A.D. 135, and is accounted for by the historian Eusebius, Bishop of Caesarea. In 212 Bishop Alexander had founded a library in the city, having come to Aelia from his home in Cappadocia. (This date is doubly important because it marks the beginning of recorded pilgrimage.) His contemporary, the philosopher Origen of Alexandria, also came, searching for texts and manuscripts, and, with others, to investigate the origins of the Holy Places. All this Eusebius recounts, clearly stating that the Holy Places were marked down and that this knowledge was handed down from father to son. In this they were inadvertently helped by Hadrian, who had built his temple to Venus above the tomb of Jesus, and had placed a statue of Jupiter upon Calvary. He had also planted a grove of trees, sacred tô Adonis, around the cave at Bethlehem, within which the early Christians believed Jesus to have been born. Thus he greatly facilitated the task of identifying and reclaiming these Holy Places at a later date.

Although knowledge of these early years is scant, it is certain that during the second half of the century the final links with Judaism were severed, under the persecutions of Diocletian and Galerius. The brief regrouping of Gentile Christians in Jerusalem and Palestine was virtually terminated, and would not begin again to augment the few who remained until the Emperor Constantine granted religious liberty to the western Christians in A.D. 313 by the edict of Milan, and in Palestine in A.D. 324. Thus, Christianity was to return not to Herod's city but to a new Roman city with a population composed of Greeks, Romans, and the non-Jewish inhabitants of Syria Palestina.

Arch with frescoes, and silver lamp on Orthodox Calvary.

The Byzantine Period (324 to 638)

The Constantinian Era (324 to 337)

The order of imperial succession was clear in theory, but, as often happens, individuals sometimes considered that their own claims could be pressed with advantage. When Diocletian in the East and Maximinian in the West both retired, no fewer than six

Franciscan monks officiating on Calvary.

contenders sought to rule the empire. By A.D. 312 Constantine, son of Augustus Constantius Chlorus, had become master of the West, having defeated Maxentius near Rome. Tradition has it that he dreamed that he would conquer in the sign of the cross, and, having done so, announced his conversion to Christianity. It is not clear why he was so converted. He himself has left no explanation, and it is unlikely that a tough general of his calibre would act on a mere passing whim. Perhaps he genuinely felt that Jesus was a more powerful God than Apollo or Hercules, his own patrons. Some say that his conversion was lightly held, pointing out that he was baptised only on his death-bed. But this in itself was not unusual at the time, since the church taught that baptism washed away all sin. Therefore, a prudent man might be tempted to wait for this absolving sacrament until he felt sure that he would sin no more, and could thus enter his spiritual life unblemished. But ambiguities persist: the Sun of Apollo remained on Constantine's coins, and he attributed his critical victory over Licinius in 324, which made him ruler of the East as well, to *instinctu divinitatis* — but omitted to say whether Jesus or Apollo, his former patron, was the source of this divine inspiration. Constantine's acceptance of the Christian God has, however, been most emphatically stated by the late Professor N. H. Baynes (*Cambridge Ancient History*, Volume 12). It is worth quoting his authoritative opinion:

Against the advice of the augurs, in spite of his military counsellors, unsupported by the troops of Licinius, with incredible audacity Constantine had risked everything on a single hazard — and won. How shall that success be explained? Constantine himself knew well the reason for his victory: it had been won by instinctu divinitatis, *by a* virtus *which was no mere human valour, but was a mysterious force which had its origin in God . . . Victory had been promised him by the God of the Christians; he had challenged the Christian God to an Ordeal by Battle and that God had kept his pledge. This belief of Constantine remains of fundamental significance for the understanding of the policy of the reign.*

Greek crosses from Mount Athos (1766) containing carved wooden miniature scenes from the life of Christ.

Be that as it may, the record stands, and we should accept Constantine at his own word. In an ecclesiastical dispute which he was to judge, he asked why judgement should be asked of him, who also waited upon judgement by Christ. He believed himself to be ''God's man'' and described Christianity as being ''the struggle for deathlessness''.

Under Constantine, the first day of the week became a holiday, ''The Sun's Day'', reflecting his Nordic heritage and our own Anglo-Saxon Sunday, as opposed to the Mediterranean peoples' *Dimanche, Domingo, Domenica,* or ''Lord's Day''. Privileges, once enjoyed only by pagan cults, governing such matters as tax relief and property ownership, were extended to Christianity, as was the manumission of slaves in a church. But slavery itself was not abolished. Shrewdly, Constantine did not try to impose Christianity upon the majority of his subjects, but recognized religious plurality, remaining *pontifex maximus* (chief priest) of other cults. For their part, Christians hailed with enthusiasm the new régime, and the philosophy that Empire and Church, founded almost simultaneously, reconciled man with God under political unity. Christians could happily profess one God, one Faith, one Emperor, while Constantine

Embroidered panel of an Orthodox bishop's chasuble.

renewed Hadrian's edict forbidding Jews to enter Aelia Capitolina.

In 325 Constantine presided over the first of the great doctrinal conferences of the church. The Council of Nicaea was called to settle the Arian controversy, so called because a theologian called Arius contended that Jesus Christ had been created, had changed, and was therefore subject to change. His view was contested by a deacon, Athanasius, who clearly stated that man's eternal salvation is jeopardized if the relationship between the Father and Son is not eternal and therefore unchangeable; that humanity and divinity are not so separate as to be incapable of conjunction; that if God became man in Christ, then man, to a degree, could reach God through the same Christ. Above all, Athanasius contended, Christ was fully human while retaining his eternal, unchangeable divinity. The Arians, quoting Paul's epistle to the Colossians, also maintained that Christ was "the first-born of all creation" and were not pleased to have their arguments, which were sincerely held and worthy of serious consideration, described as "unworthy of men of sense".

Constantine was dismayed by the controversy, and perplexed as well, not least because of its disruptive effect upon the stabilizing religion of his empire (even the dockers of Alexandria backed Arius with what is now called "industrial action"). The Council decided in favour of the Athanasians, having defined the relationship between the Father and the Son as "consubstantial", forming with the Holy Spirit The Trinity.

It can be appreciated that there was to be no easy answer to this controversy. Ten years later, a synod met at Tyre and reversed the Nicaean decision. The argument continued, with Arius by now dead, and Athanasius exiled.

A practical reason for the reversal of the decision of Nicaea is not hard to find, for the Arians, particularly as represented by Bishop Eusebius, were prepared to accept schismatics back into the structure of the church, while the Athanasians were not. For Constantine, unity of empire was of prime, one could even say sole, importance, but it is charitable as well as reasonable to explain his own apparent ambivalence towards Christianity and paganism by the logic that the Sun of Apollo, *Sol Invictus*, his family's heraldic device, could also represent the Sun of Righteousness, "risen with healing in his wings"; Sun-Day, the Lord's day, could symbolize the Light of the World, newly born. Thus, through careful representation and transition, could Constantine offer a diplomatic and acceptable lead towards a new monotheistic religion in which he believed, but which had yet to attract more than a tiny percentage of the people of his empire.

Ultimately, his dream of a new empire guided by the Christian God was realized. He built a new city and administrative centre for the eastern part of the empire on the Bosphorus in A.D. 330: Constantinople, erected on the site of the ancient colony of Byzantium. When the western empire lapsed into decadence and decay, and the barbarians started to close in on Rome, the eastern empire shone with splendour, and Jerusalem once more rose upon Hadrian's pagan foundations.

Constantine died on 22nd May 337. It is fitting that he should be buried in the church dedicated to the twelve apostles, for if Saint Paul and others had broadcast the seed of Christianity throughout the civilized Roman world, it was Constantine who had cultivated and tilled the soil, that the seed might flourish.

A Greek priest.

Good Friday: Greek priests at the Unction Stone performing the ceremony of Anointing the Body of Christ.

The Constantinian Basilica

At the Council of Nicaea, Constantine met and came to know well the Bishop of Aelia, Makarios. The latter sought to take away the primacy of Palestine from Caesarea and to restore his bishopric of Aelia to the first rank. He was not successful in this, but he did obtain permission for the destruction of Hadrian's Temple of Venus in order to rediscover the Tomb of Jesus and the site of the Crucifixion. Makarios undertook this search unhesitatingly, and succeeded, showing how strong was the verbal tradition handed down from generation to generation, and how well the site had been preserved beneath Hadrian's temple.

Constantine was delighted by the news and immediately gave instructions to Makarios for the erection of a magnificent church upon the site: "... it is your task to ensure that everything is done in order that this edifice shall not only be the most beautiful in the world ... Our piety has commanded us to have put at your disposal the necessary artists, workmen, and in general all means... Send me the designs for the columns and marble that you consider most precious and suitable."

In that same year, 326, Constantine's mother, Helena, arrived in Aelia, probably bearing instructions from her son, the Emperor, but also upon her own pilgrimage. When her husband Constantius Chlorus had become emperor, she had been divorced in order that he could marry Theodora, the step-daughter of the Emperor Maximian. Later she had her personal triumph when her son Constantine was proclaimed emperor by the legions in Britain. She had been converted to Christianity at the age of sixty-five, after Constantine's dream of the conquering sign of the cross. Shortly before her arrival in Rome, Constantine had been persuaded through the deceit of his second wife Fausta into executing his son Crispus. Helena was greatly affected by the death of her favourite grandson.

The Patriarch Makarios received his royal visitor amid general acclamation. Never before had a person of such high status — and a Christian — come to take such a personal interest in the affairs of the church; one moreover who represented the Emperor of Rome himself. Helena then set about a programme of patronage and construction which has left an indelible impression on the Holy Land. The great Basilica of the Nativity in Bethlehem, standing today in all its monumental splendour, and the Eleona Church upon the Mount of Olives, now destroyed but beneath the convent of the Pater Noster, are closely associated with her, as is the Church of the Resurrection itself. Less directly sponsored perhaps, but none the less inspired by her zeal for building, were the churches of Mary the Mother of Jesus in Nazareth, of Saint Abraham by Hebron, and a number of others in Galilee.

Helena's special quest, which dated from the time of her son's prophetic dream, was to find the cross upon which Christ had been crucified. In this, we are told, she succeeded, although Eusebius, that most pertinacious of historians, makes no mention of so important an event. Tradition has it that amongst the debris found in a cistern, between the tomb, Calvary, and the Old City Wall, were the remains of three crosses. This would not be remarkable in itself, for the area about the former execution ground would be bound to retain such relics in profusion, and cisterns, or even the fosse outside the wall, would have been filled up at the time of the city's destruction. However, by the placing

Greek cross of John Palologus (1440) containing fragments of the True Cross. This side is encrusted with rubies.

The Aedicule of the Tomb of Christ. (The scaffolding is now being removed.)

of each cross in turn ·upon a dying woman, the miracle of a sudden and dramatic recovery gave clear indication to Helena which was the cross of Christ. Thus, the "true" cross was identified, together with the nails which fastened the body of Christ to it. These naturally became relics of the utmost importance.

In Madaba, above the eastern shores of the Dead Sea, are many relics of early Christian occupation, none more famous than its mosaic floors. Most renowned of all is the map of Palestine, dating from the sixth century, which, although obliterated in part, shows an extremely clear plan of Aelia Capitolina. Dominant within it is the Basilica of the Holy Sepulchre. The Cardo Maximus is clearly seen as well. But before describing the great complex we should consider the topography.

At the time of the crucifixion, the land to the west of the city wall was pitted with tombs and quarries, and somewhat higher than the level of the city. This necessitated the building of a defensive *fossa* (ditch) outside the wall. A knoll or hillock was part of this rising ground, and offered an admirable place upon which to display executed malefactors to all who went in and out of the city by the Ephraim Gate, By law, no one could be buried inside the city, and it was customary for the more well-to-do to have their tombs prepared for them as near to the gateway as possible. There, the earth is rich and reddish, and, although not a "garden" in the European sense, is fertile enough to support the growth of cultivated olives and vines. The quarry pits themselves would be used as cisterns to conserve the rainfall much needed by an expanding city. It was upon this open ground that Hadrian placed the platform for his forum and the Temple of Venus, leaving the top of the hillock of Calvary as a base for his statue of Jupiter. Constantine's workmen removed the platform of the Temple and found the tomb beneath it surprisingly intact: a double chamber hewn out of the rock, with a rolling stone to cover the entrance. First of all, the rock all round the tomb was cut away and levelled, leaving it like a hollow cone in the middle of a circular space. Next, the hill of Calvary was trimmed down to a base size of 4·5 metres by 4·5 metres, leaving its height at about 11 metres. The tomb was enclosed by a small aedicule with twelve columns, inset into the western end of a level platform or atrium. Towards the end of the fourth century, the colonnaded Rotunda or Anastasis, about 30 metres in diameter, was completed over the Tomb upon the western part. It had three recesses, at its northern, western and southern points. This is called the Anastasis (Place of Resurrection). The little hill of Calvary was left free standing, its rock bedecked and surmounted by a jewelled and decorated cross, at the southern side of the inner Atrium or Cloister.

To the east of this was the main Martyrion or Basilica. This was sumptuously decorated with gold, silver and magnificent marble columns. It was 45 metres long, 26 metres wide, and comprised five naves, with an apse at the western end. Beneath it, as a crypt, lay the Chapel of the Invention (or Finding) of the Cross, dedicated to Saint Helena, and reached by a grand stairway. To the eastward side again was the outer Atrium, which was approached from the street up five steps and through a triple gateway built into the earlier second north wall of the city. All this can be clearly seen in the Madaba mosaic map, together with the Triple Gateway, or Propylaea. Remnants of this gateway and of the columns taken from Hadrian's Temple and the Cardo Maximus in Constantine's building are still visible, behind what is now a pastry shop,

Embroidered panel of a Greek episcopal dress.

The Tomb of Christ. The altar and the marble-encased shelf upon which the Body reposed.

in the Convent of Alexandros Nefki (The Russian Excavations), and beneath the Coptic Monastery (Deir el-Sultan). To the south of the inner Atrium and Anastasis (or Rotunda) were a Baptistry and associated buildings. These could be approached down a flight of steps from the street which is now called Christian Street. It is thought that part of this street may well lie upon another section of the elusive second north wall. This most significant Church of the Resurrection was officially consecrated on 13th September 335 in the presence of 300 bishops from all over the Christian world, and was to remain resplendent until it was utterly destroyed by the Persians in 614.

The Byzantine Era 337 to 638

Aelia Capitolina became once more the Holy City of Jerusalem. Beyond the confines of its boundaries, prosperity returned with the pilgrims, and two hundred years of peace. But if all was peaceful in the outside world, controversy raged within the Church, as it sought to find itself during the period of its adolescence.

On Constantine's death, the empire was divided among his three sons, of whom Constantius held the eastern part. He and his people followed the Arian doctrine, while his brothers in the central and western empire held to the original Athanasian or Nicaean concept (after the Council of Nicaea) of the Trinity. After the death of one in battle against his brother, and the subsequent murder of the survivor, Constantius became sole Emperor. Saint Jerome, succinct as always in his commentary, observed: "The world woke up one day to find itself Arian."

Thus began, or rather continued, the unedifying pattern of banishment of the bishops of whichever persuasion was in opposition to the reigning emperor. However, both sects were agreed that their religious squabble had nothing to do with the emperor of the day, nor should he intervene in doctrinal issues.

Constantius died in 361 and was succeeded by his cousin, Julian, known as "the Apostate". Brought up as a Christian, he was also a Platonist who believed that the gods of old emanated from the Universal Being. His position, while technically neutral towards Christianity, was important because it allowed the return to power of the Orthodox Nicene bishops. He died two years later in 363, and the controversy raged until 381. In that year the Spanish Emperor Theodosius I (379–395) summoned the Second Ecumenical Council to Constantinople and not only reaffirmed the original decision of Nicaea, but forbade all forms of heretical or pagan worship. His successor, Theodosius II, in 438 went further still, when he decreed the death penalty upon those who denied the Trinity (the Arians).

This period was also a time of great monastic expansion throughout the Holy Land, and the controversy was hotly debated within the many convents set up around such distinguished teachers as Saint Savvas (Mar Saba), Saint Basil, Saint Theodosius and Saint Theogeos. The most famous of all was Saint Jerome, because of his translation of the Bible from Hebrew and Greek into Latin, now known as the Vulgate.

Pilgrims flocked from all over the world: Ethiopians, Persians, Greeks, Latins, Egyptians (whose church is thought to have been founded as early as A.D. 40 by Saint Mark himself), Armenians, Syrians, Indians, and others from the cold reaches of Europe. The

Armenian chalice of gold and silver filigree, encrusted with jewels (Constantinople, 1755).

Oil lamps, belonging to the Eastern Orthodox, Armenian and Latin churches, above the entrance to the Tomb.

monastic movement was encouraged by a rejection to the degree of secularization which had been infused into religion under the official Theodosian Code, and the removal of the threat of persecution led to the seeking of other heroic ways in which faith might be proved and sin expiated. The cruel and waterless desert offered not only sanctuary for the dissenters, but a merciless environment in which to test the strongest resolution.

In A.D. 410 Rome fell. The shock of this event in the East was as much psychological as political, for Rome had been the indestructible centre of the known world, the very core of history and order. But Constantinople was to remain, vigorous and proud, for centuries to come; the capital of an empire secure in the faith which it would one day return to Rome, to reinstate Rome as the centre of the Church Eternal on earth.

In spite of this, the arguments about the nature of Christ and the form of his relationship to God and the Holy Spirit continued unabated. Inevitably, practical politico-geographic factors imposed themselves both in proposition and in resolution. The Syrian, Armenian, Georgian, and Coptic (Egyptian) communities found themselves alienated by distance and language from the Greeks of Byzantium, and when Nestorius became bishop of Constantinople in 428, fresh controversy broke out. At Nicaea it had been affirmed that Christ and God were consubstantial, but the Apostles' Creed also declared Christ to be Man. Therefore, how was his divinity related to his humanity? Furthermore, Nestorius considered Mary to be the Mother of Christ only, not of God, even though Christ and God were one under the Nicene doctrine. At the Third Ecumenical Council at Ephesus in 431, Nestorius was outvoted and condemned by the bishops of both Alexandria and Rome. He was exiled to Persia.

Later, a thesis was postulated by a Greek monk called Eutyches which further confused the issue. This was the doctrine of Monophysitism (one nature) according to which the divinity of Christ was total and absolute, and his human form illusory. At the Fourth Ecumenical Council at Chalcedon in 451, this view was rejected, and it was again confirmed that Christ was both human and divine, inseparable yet separate. This position has been generally accepted by the Orthodox churches ever since.*

The Copts retained their Monophysite position, transmitting it to the Ethiopians; so did the Syrian Jacobite church, named after Jacob Baradi, of which the members were known as Melkites: followers of the Melik (Emperor) of Constantinople. The Nestorians held fast in Syria, and sent their missionaries as far east as China. The Armenians, the earliest nation to adopt Christianity (in A.D. 300), accepted Monophysitism as being a neutral position between those of the rival empires of Byzantium and Persia. The Georgians remained loyal to Orthodoxy.

Fresco panel on an arch of Orthodox Calvary.

"The Holy Orthodox Eastern Church, which embraces the four historic Patriarchates of Constantinople, Alexandria, Antioch, and Jerusalem, together with the national churches of Russia, Greece, Yugoslavia, Bulgaria, Rumania, is often miscalled the 'Greek Orthodox Church'. The only body correctly so called is the part of it under the jurisdiction of the Holy Synod of the Kingdom of Greece. The Patriarchate of Jerusalem, with a two-fold mission, the custody of the Orthodox share of the Holy Places and the spiritual oversight of the Palestinian Orthodox Arabs, has a Greek Hierarchy and an Arab parochial clergy. The liturgical language of each branch of the Orthodox Church is the vernacular of the country." Stewart Perowne, *In Jerusalem and Bethlehem*, Hodder & Stoughton, 1964.

Easter Saturday: Ethiopian ceremony of Searching for the Body of Christ.

A most colourful and dramatic lady had by now entered Jerusalem's history. In 438 the Empress Eudocia, wife of Theodosius II, visited Jerusalem. On her return to Constantinople, after donating towards the building of new churches, she was displaced in court circles by her sister-in-law because of her Greek origin. Only part of one of her churches remains, as the crypt of the small church of Saint John Prodromos (the Baptist), in austere and moving trifoliate simplicity.

In 441 she fled from Constantinople after her adviser had been killed by her husband on suspicion of a more intimate relationship. She was pursued by an officer who, acting on Theodosius's instructions, murdered her counsellor-priest and his deacon. In rage and fury, she herself slew the assassin. Exiled to Palestine, under surprisingly amicable and generous terms, she was to become its virtual ruler until her death in 460. Her generosity and her zeal for building were immense. She supervised the rebuilding of the walls of the city in the face of the growing threat from the Persians and the Huns, and to her is ascribed the construction of the Golden Gate that we see today. Churches, palaces, hostels: "The blessed Eudocia constructed for Christ a great number of churches and so many monasteries and hospices for the poor and aged that I cannot enumerate them all." So wrote a contemporary chronicler.

But in matters of theology she was less skilled or less fortunate. The Council of Chalcedon had upgraded the Bishopric of Jerusalem to a Patriarchate in its own right. Its bishop, Juvenal, formerly a Monophysite, bowed to Orthodoxy in exchange for his elevation. On his return to Jerusalem, he was confronted by a rival bishop, elected by command of the Empress and by the majority of the city's Monophysite inhabitants. Eventually, a battle was fought near Nablus, following a massacre of Orthodox supporters, and Eudocia fled to Syria. After consulting Saint Euthymius, who had previously sheltered Juvenal in his desert monastery, she returned and submitted herself to the newly installed patriarch, along with a considerable number of her followers. She died three years later. In the turmoil of her life and times can be seen the beginning of political disintegration. Passion and romanticism, emotional impetuousness, coupled with old political rivalries in controversial religious guise, were beginning to point to the end of Byzantium. But at this time, the empire in the east was nearing its zenith.

The conflict over Monophysitism continued to divide the empire internally. In 484 the Emperor Zeno issued an edict in favour of the Monophysites, thereby intensifying the division within the Church. However, Jerusalem, removed from the front line of intellectual and administrative affairs, continued to grow in wealth and prosperity as the custodian city of the Holy Places and Relics.

But even within Palestine all was not well, and a series of revolts by the Samaritans involved much slaughter and bloodshed between them and the Christians. Material poverty and disorder had spread below the glittering surface, and the advent of Justinian to the imperial throne in 525 increased the persecution of the remaining Jews and non-Christians in the countryside.

However, Justinian had a more pressing problem demanding his attention. Much of the western empire had been occupied by the barbarians. He set about the reconquest of these lost territories, and a new national consciousness spread throughout the land as the Mediterranean once more became *Mare Nostrum*.

Armenian episcopal mitre.

Christ Ascending: the only remaining fragment of Frankish mosaic set in the ceiling of Latin Calvary.

In 543, Justinian gathered pilgrims and notables from all over the world to Jerusalem for the dedication of his great new church to "Saint Mary, Mother of God, and ever Virgin", the church now known as Saint Mary-the-New. Here was Jerusalem at its most magnificent. Radiating from Constantine's superb basilica of the Church of the Resurrection, the great Byzantine buildings crowded the city and the landscape, spreading out across Palestine. Never again would so many Christian sites be marked by churches of such architectural importance. Processions moving from all around towards the Holy Sepulchre were colourful threads within the rich tapestry of Jerusalem. Here was the triumphant climax to the history of the first Christian city.

Justinian's death in 565 marked the beginning of the end. In spite of his efforts to resuscitate it, the Roman Empire was doomed. Italy lay devastated and was soon overwhelmed except in the extreme south. Spain fell to the Visigoths, who had swept down through Europe, and the victorious Berbers in North Africa were to be joined within seventy years by the sweeping armies of the Arabs, streaming west from their desert heartland. But for Justinian's own epitaph it can be written that under him and his laws, the Justinian Code, shape and form had been given to Byzantine culture, which has remained one of the most vibrant and splendid aspects of human history.

After Justinian's death, King Chosroes II of Persia took advantage of a revolution within the empire and attacked westward in 606, reaching the Bosphorus in 609. Heraclius, a stalwart provincial governor from Africa, seized the throne in 610, and began to organize resistance and counter-attack. But on 20th May 614, Jerusalem fell to Chosroes. It seems that a few weeks after its initial surrender, the Persian governor was assassinated, and in retaliation a tremendous slaughter of its inhabitants and massive destruction took place. In this, the invading Persians were willingly assisted by the Jewish inhabitants of Palestine, 26,000 of whom had joined their army in order to revenge themselves for all their years of suppression. The Church of the Resurrection was destroyed and the desecration was absolute. Fires raged through all the churches, and a pitiful column of survivors set out into captivity. They were accompanied by the holiest of all relics; the True Cross in its silver case; a gift for the Nestorian Queen of Persia.

Heraclius did not give up in spite of the defeat of his southern flank. He attacked deep into Persian-held territory, forcing Chosroes to pull back until the latter died when he himself was encamped before Ctesiphon. Heraclius concluded a treaty with Chosroes' son in 629, by which he recovered his provinces, his prisoners and the Cross. Returning in triumph to the ruins of Jerusalem, he dismounted before the Golden Gate, put off his finery and accoutrements, and carried the Holy Relic barefoot back to the Church of the Resurrection. This date is celebrated on 14th September, the Feast of the Exaltation of the Cross.

Inside the city, between its sacking and the return of the Cross in 629, some repair work had been carried out. Although the Persians remained masters of the country until the peace treaty was signed, Modestus, the abbot of the monastery of Saint Theodosius, was allowed and able to undertake certain functional repairs. Funds were collected principally from John "The Almoner", Patriarch of Alexandria, and the aedicule of the Sepulchre was repaired. The Anastasis was fitted with a new dome and

An Armenian bishop.

Holy Fire!

the Martyrion reroofed, but there was none of the elaborate decorative work to replace that which had been irrevocably destroyed. For his efforts and achievement, Modestus was confirmed as Patriarch of Jerusalem.

Jerusalem never recovered her former glory. The short period of reconstruction was to last only until 638 — eight brief years. Worn out by their wars, Byzantium and Persia lay bankrupt and exhausted. In 633 the Emperor Heraclius removed the Holy Relic of the Cross when he withdrew to Constantinople, leaving Jerusalem depleted and exposed. The new threat was to come not from the north or the east, but from the south, tearing like a whirlwind out of the deserts of Arabia, spurred on by religious zeal and bearing the message of God's last prophet on earth, Muhammad, under the banners of the Caliph Omar Ibn Al-Khattab and his general Khaled Ibn Al-Walid.*

Illuminated page of plainsong manuscript given to Franciscan monks by John of Gaunt.

Muslim Jerusalem (638 to 1099)

The Arabs encamped before Jerusalem two years after defeating a Byzantine army at the River Yarmuk in 636. The city was surrendered in 638 by its Patriarch Sophronius upon generous terms. Unlike previous conquerors, Omar did not seek the destruction of the city, which he and his armies considered holy. The Jews had been expelled again by Heraclius for their part in the destruction of the city in 614, but Omar allowed the Christian inhabitants their freedom of religion and possessions, and they were obliged to pay tax in lieu of military service. Certain other measures affecting internal security were enforced, such as prohibitions on carrying arms and on riding astride on horseback; and the monasteries had to submit to inspection since they could, by the nature of their construction, have been used as strongpoints.

Having refused to pray in the Church of the Holy Sepulchre, lest his followers should subsequently turn it into a mosque, Omar concentrated his efforts on clearing the deserted site of the old temple to reveal and cleanse the Sacred Rock of Abraham. From this rock, Muslims believe, Muhammad had been escorted up to heaven by the Archangel Gabriel to receive divine instructions. He had miraculously flown thither from Mecca, and returned there before dawn (Holy Quran, Sura XVII).

Counting Jesus among the great prophets of the Bible, the Muslims respected the tradition of both Jews and Christians as being "people of the book". However, they considered that misinterpretation of and deviation from God's original instructions made both religions inadequate, and that only by strict observance of the revelations made to His Last Prophet could true obedience be achieved and salvation granted. In the Faith of Islam, the gospel account of Jesus' birth is considered true, and it is believed that He will preside over the Last Judgement upon the Mount of Olives. Special status is given to Mary, the saintliest of women. "How shall I bear a child," she asked the messenger of the Lord, "when I am a virgin, untouched by man?" (Holy Quran, Sura XIX). Furthermore, the Quran states that Jesus ascended into Heaven (Sura IV).

* See *The Noble Sanctuary*, Longman, 1972.

Panels from an Eastern Orthodox episcopal chasuble.

34

In 685, the ninth successor to Muhammad, the Caliph Abd' Al Malik Ibn Marawan, started to build the shrine known as the Dome of the Rock, above the Sacred Rock of Abraham. Called Al-Qubbat al-Sakhra, it is the oldest existing Islamic building and is of breathtaking beauty. It combines the best of Byzantine architecture and Islamic decorative design, and remains "as magnificent a tribute to the glory of God as can be seen anywhere in the world".*

Its gilded dome was almost identical in form to that above the Church of the Resurrection (Holy Sepulchre), but, by virtue of its setting and its lavish decoration, it was of far greater visual impact.

By and large, the situation was now tolerable for the Christians, and pilgrimage recommenced. Certainly, Bishop Arculf, a Frank, who visited Jerusalem in 670, described conditions there as being satisfactory. The state of tolerance lasted until the Omayyads were driven out by the Abbasids, descendants of the Prophet's uncle Al-Abbas. Subsequent caliphs from successive dynasties did little to promote the well-being of the Christian community. At best it was tolerated or ignored.

In 746 an earthquake struck Jerusalem, doing great damage to the city and to the Church of the Resurrection, thus further straining the city's meagre resources. Luckily, the Caliph Haroun Al-Rashid, who was campaigning against Byzantium, agreed to enter into a political treaty with Charlemagne, king of a newly constituted alliance between the Papacy and the Franks — a new Roman Empire in the west. In exchange for Holy Relics, Charlemagne sent money for sustenance, repairs and reconstruction to Jerusalem. It is doubtful if he ever received the keys of the Church of the Resurrection as it is sometimes alleged. The overall outcome, in any case, was that Latin as opposed to Orthodox foundations were established in the Holy City.

The Eastern Empire was still harrowed by old and new controversies. While it had expended more energy and effort over the Sixth Ecumenical Council at Constantinople in 680, which sought to re-establish the Monophysites in the interest of political strength, it seemingly failed to appreciate that these people had already, for the most part, been conquered by the banners of Islam.

Since earliest times, the adoration of icons or personal images had been an accepted Christian practice. Now the "Iconoclasts", as they were called, made objection to this, claiming that it amounted to idolatry. Riots and upheavals broke out across the empire as to the acceptance or rejection of physical representation as an aid to faith and spiritual symbolism. Inevitably, the Seventh Ecumenical Council met once more at Nicaea in 787, and the "images" were restored to respectability, providing that the relief or indenture was not so great as to enable a nose to be held between forefinger and thumb.

One may well marvel at such apparent trivia being given all this attention at a time of peril. But such controversies refined the essential element of the Eastern Church, reinforcing its pride and its claim to be the true custodian of Orthodox Christianity and the classical heritage. If Byzantium was unable to destroy or convert the Arabs, it did,

An Armenian episcopal chasuble.

Mediaeval illuminated Coptic Testament showing Saint Mark and the beginning of his Gospel.

* See *The Noble Sanctuary*, Longman, 1972.

ⲡⲉⲩⲁⲅⲅⲉⲗⲓⲟⲛ ⲉⲑⲟⲩ
ⲕⲁⲧⲁ ⲙⲁⲣⲭⲟⲛ

ⲦⲀⲢⲬⲎ ⲘⲠⲈⲬⲀ
ⲄⲄⲈⲖⲒⲞⲚⲎⲈⲒⲎⲤ

ⲙ̄ⲡ̄ⲭ̄ⲥ̄ ⲡϣⲏⲣⲓ
ⲙ̄ⲫⲏⲟⲩⲧⲉ
ⲙ̄ⲫⲣⲏϯ ⲉⲧⲥϧⲏⲟⲩⲧ
ⲫⲣⲟⲫⲏⲧⲏⲥ
ϫⲉ ⲟⲩⲣⲡⲓ ⲡⲁⲁⲅⲅⲉⲗⲟⲥ
ⲉⲛⲓⲡⲉⲭ̄ ⲟ ⲫⲛⲉⲃⲓⲁⲥⲟ
ⲡⲉⲕⲙ̄ⲑⲟ ... ⲉ ⲑⲁⲙⲓⲟ
ⲡⲉⲕⲙⲱⲓⲧ
ⲡⲣⲱⲙⲓ ⲡⲉⲧⲱϣ ⲉⲃⲟⲗ
ⲩⲉ ⲭⲉⲥ ⲃ̄ ⲧⲉⲫϣⲁϥⲉ
ⲥⲟⲃⲧ ⲙ̄ⲡⲉϥⲙⲱⲓⲧ
ⲁϥϣⲱⲡⲓ ⲛϫⲉ ⲓⲱⲁⲛⲛⲏⲥ
ⲣⲉϥϯⲱⲙⲥ ⲙ̄ⲡ... ⲉ ⲑ̄ⲃ̄
ⲟⲩⲟ ⲛⲟⲩⲧⲱⲙⲥ ⲙ̄ⲡⲉⲧⲁⲛⲟⲓⲁ
ⲉⲡⲭⲱ ⲉⲃⲟⲗ ⲛ̄ⲛⲓⲛⲟⲃⲓ
ⲟⲩⲟ ⲛⲁⲩⲛⲏⲟⲩ ⲉⲃⲟⲗ ϩⲁⲣⲟϥ ⲛ̄
ⲙⲁϥⲛⲓⲟⲩⲇⲉⲁ ⲧⲏⲣⲥ ⲛ̄ⲭⲱⲣⲁ

بشارة القديس مرقس
الانجيل
المسيح ابن الله
كما هو مكتوب في
الانبياء هوذا
ارسل ملاكي امام
وجهك يعظم طريقك
قدامك
صوت صارخ في
البرية اعدوا طريق
الرب وسهلوا سبله
كان يوحنا المعمد
في البرية يبشر
بمعمودية التوبة
لغفران الخطايا
وكان يخرج اليه
كل كور اليهودية

in time, pass on to them the best of this heritage, which, coupled with the arts and culture learnt from the East, was to be transmitted back to Europe via Spain and the Renaissance.

While the new Latin Christian Empire in the West sought diplomatic alliance with the Abbasid Caliphs against their mutual enemy, the Orthodox Christian Empire in the East, the latter continued sporadic attempts to recover land lost to the Muslims. At the same time, weakening Abbasid control enabled local governors to pursue independent courses of their own whim or for their own benefit, and Palestine witnessed more local oppression of its Christian people and destruction of their property. In 966, probably in revenge for Byzantine campaigning far away in the north, the Patriarch John VII was murdered by Muslims and the Church of the Resurrection was pillaged once more. In 967 Jews and Muslims set fire to the church and burnt down the Patriarchate. Finally, in 969 the rule of the Abbasids was superseded by the Fatimids, originally from North Africa, who took over the seat of power in Baghdad. In 975, taking advantage of this dispute, the Emperor Nicephorus Phocas advanced east and southward. The northern half of Palestine was briefly recaptured by his general John Timiskes, long enough for a prior claim to the whole land to be established when, later, the First Crusade was to roll down towards Jerusalem. The Byzantines withdrew on the death of the Emperor in 976, and the Fatimids resumed an understandably more severe control of the Holy Land.

In 996, Al-Hakim Bi Amrillah ascended to the Caliphate. Born of a Christian mother, and most charitably described as "eccentric", he was a Shiite Muslim, fanatically impassioned, who showed no mercy or toleration towards his people, Muslim or Christian. In 1009, upon the pretext, not unreasonably founded, that the annual ceremony of the Miracle of the Holy Fire was fraudulently contrived and a deception of the people, he ordered his army ". . . to destroy the Church of the Resurrection, to the very roots, and to pull up its illustrious foundations . . ." Only the broken base of the tomb remained. Golgotha, or rather the decoration that was set upon the rock, was stripped bare, and everything within the precincts of the Church was looted and destroyed. In 1034 the last and final destruction of the Church was accomplished by earthquake. A similar fate befell the rest of Christian Palestine, and thousands fled. Towards the end of his life the Caliph mellowed somewhat towards Christianity, allowing apostates to Islam to revert to Christianity, and permitting property to be returned to the Church. The Patriarch Nicephorus was allowed to resume his office, while Al-Hakim turned his murderous attentions towards his own Muslim people nearer home. In 1021 he disappeared suddenly, and was presumed to be dead, but by what means or where, nobody knows. To this day the Druze people of southern Syria and Lebanon believe in his claim to have been a divine manifestation of God and await his return to earth.

Byzantium now set about re-establishing itself in Jerusalem. A treaty was made *circa* 1037, and a large indemnity was paid over to the Fatimids in return for official recognition of Byzantine custodianship of the Holy Places. When Constantine (IX) Monomachus became emperor in 1042 (his name means "gladiator") the work of reconstruction commenced. By 1048 the Anastasis had been rebuilt and decorated

Panel of Greek episcopal chasuble.

Illuminated Greek Testament of the sixteenth century, showing the beginning of Saint Luke's Gospel.

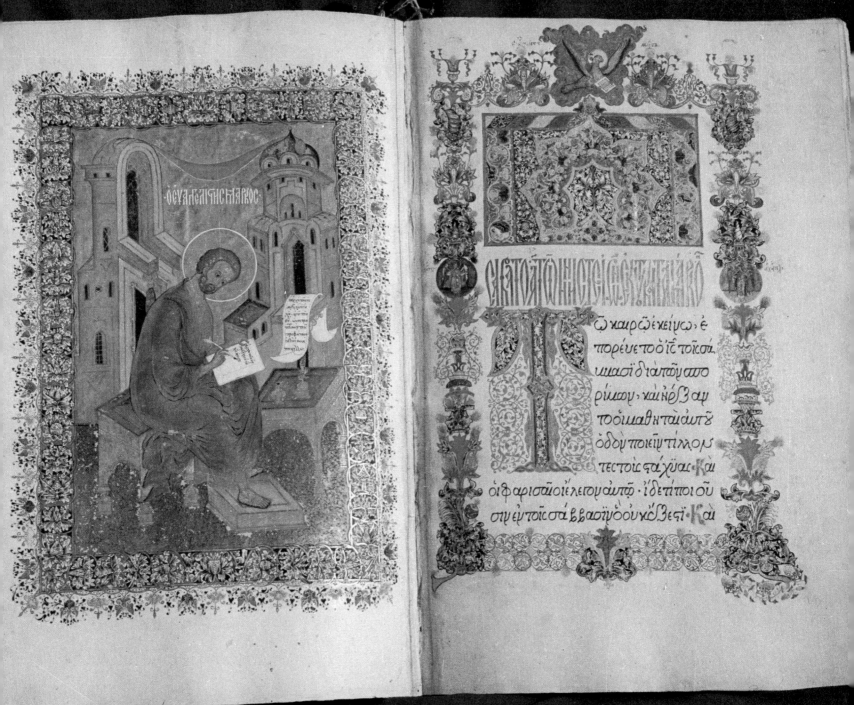

with mosaics, and a small chapel and enclosure built around and over Calvary. Four chapels flanked the Anastasis: to Saint Mary the Virgin, Saint John, Saint James, and the Holy Trinity. A small chapel was erected above the crypt of the Invention (Finding) of the Cross, and an Atrium or court was laid out between this and Calvary. Further shrines are thought to have adjoined this Atrium, such as the Prison of Christ, the place of Mocking of Christ and the Division of his Raiment, and a stone, the Ompholos, which marked the Centre of the Earth. The Martyrion remained untouched. Across the street lay the churches of Saint Mary the Latin and Saint Mary the Less. These descriptions come from Seawulf, an Englishman who became a monk at Malmesbury, and Daniel, a Russian abbot, both of whom visited Jerusalem, in 1102 and 1106 respectively. At that date, no new work of restoration had been begun by the Crusaders.

It can be clearly seen that this third reconstruction was even more modest and incomplete than that of Modestus's time.

The next forty years were peaceful, and pilgrimages resumed. During this time, Christians moved into their own quarter of the city, where before they had been interspersed among the Muslim population. Byzantium was stronger, so the Fatimids took care not to oppress the Christian community too much. In 1063 merchants from Amalfi, with considerable trade connections in the Levant, were permitted to finance the construction of a small church and a hospital for pilgrims. This was later to become the foundation church of the great military order of knights, the Hospitallers of Saint John.

Now the time had arrived for the prologue to the great Christian re-entry into the Holy Land. In 1071 the Seljuk Turks poured out of Asia under their Sultan Alp Arslan. They defeated the Byzantines decisively at Manzikert in Armenia and captured the Emperor Diogenes. They took over the leadership of Islam, and captured Jerusalem in 1077 and Nicaea a year later. Once more Christian faced Muslim across the narrow Bosphorus. Terrified refugees streamed west, bearing horrifying tales of persecution, although Jerusalem itself was spared slaughter. The Egyptian Fatimids regained a tenuous occupation of the city in 1098, and were to form the luckless garrison when the Crusaders crashed through the walls the following year. Faced with a massive threat at his very doorstep, the Byzantine Emperor Alexius Comnenos appealed to Western Christendom for help.

A Coptic priest.

The First Crusade* (1099 to 1187)

Religious issues are rarely used by themselves as reasons for precipitating a country into war. We know this full well, and in the eleventh century, those engaged in the exercise of political power were no more inclined to rely on them than a modern politician would be. Certainly, public opinion had to be moulded to the support of a political decision, and what better way of stirring and marshalling that support than by a cause which combined romanticism and religious fervour with opportunity for

* Generally so called, but technically Heraclius's campaign of 622 holds precedence.

Mediaeval Coptic pilgrim-conductor's badge, worn on the sleeve.

personal advancement and material gain? But before we listen to what the Arab historian Philip Hitti described as "probably the most effective speech in history", let us consider the European situation as it existed in 1095, of which an appreciation was made by the political leaders of the Western alliance to justify going to war:

1. Western Latin forces were successfully campaigning against the Muslim incursion into Europe; Sicily and southern Italy had been recovered; Spain was in process of recovery but still posed a threat. The Mediterranean was at last becoming *Mare Nostrum* again.
2. Internal dissension between the Sunni and Shi'a sects of Islam and the intervention of the Sunni Seljuk Turks were bound to weaken the Shi'a hold over the Eastern Mediterranean and the Levant.
3. The Eastern Orthodox Empire was struggling against the Turkish onslaught in the east, and was under naval pressure from Norman forces in the Adriatic. Their empire had been excommunicated by the Pope.
4. The new young Byzantine Emperor Comnenos needed to reinforce his north-western frontiers with mercenary troops which only western Europe could supply.

Gold cover of sixteenth-century Greek Testament, encrusted with jewels.

If the Latin Franks and the Papal powers wished to reassert supremacy over the Ortho-dox Church (as representing Byzantium) and further expand their own empire and trading areas, this was an opportunity not to be missed. By allying themselves with the weakened Byzantium, they could seize control of the Holy Places, once the Muslims had been driven from Jerusalem, and place them under Latin protection. The forces of both Latins (or Franks as they came to be called) and Orthodox would then re-establish the great Christian empire; but this time with Rome and not Constantinople in effective overall command, and physically controlling both flanks of the revived empire.

To support this strategic plan, domestic conditions in Europe were helpful. There had been bad harvests of late. The towns and cities were ill-disciplined and overcrowded. Worst of all for the clergy, the knightly aristocracy was for the most part brutal, licentious, predatory and virtually uncontrollable. Their ethics, if their pattern of behaviour could be graced with such a name, were not far from those of the Norse raiders and Vikings; the chief virtues they acknowledged were physical prowess and an overdeveloped sense of revenge; their sports were rape and pillage; and their hopes were for the acquisition of lands — rich, fertile lands — such as they had won in England, France and Italy. If this sounds overemphatic or too harsh a portrait, we must also give them their due; some of these self-same men, professional soldiers if you will, were destined to forge under the banner of the Cross regiments whose discipline and control in and out of battle were to rank them with the finest troops of all time.

But to return: the mystical influence of the church over the population of Europe was considerable. For the masses, the Holy Land and "Jerusalem the Golden" of psalm and hymn were symbols of the heavenly kingdom to which they aspired and for which they yearned in a harsh and bitter world. That people described to them, quite erron-eously, as "unbelievers" should have taken control of their Holy Places was to their simple minds almost equivalent to stealing their dreams. The growing awareness of the

Panel of the mediaeval door of the Eastern Orthodox Chapel of Saint James, showing Adam, Eve and the serpent.

humanity of Jesus, combined with the threat of the physical proximity of the "Saracen unbelievers" in Spain, was a curiously explosive mixture. Those Arabic-speaking Christians and others who appreciated the higher culture of the Arabs and their great and passionate belief in their noble faith were, of course, those for whom such emotions needed to be placed in a practical context. They were concerned with trade routes, markets, balances of power, and political leverage.

In 1095, on 18th November, a council was held at Clermont under the chairmanship of Pope Urban II, which seems to have dealt exclusively with domestic matters ranging from ecclesiastical reform to the adultery of the King of France with the Countess of Anjou. But it was after the council business was concluded that Pope Urban went out and addressed a vast crowd. The great assembly could hardly have gathered by accident, nor was his speech unpremeditated. Like many an impassioned political orator, he spoke in measured tones, describing the pitiful conditions of the Holy Places and the horrible suffering of his listeners' co-religionists. His words rose to a climax: ". . . need it is indeed to hasten to your eastern brothers . . ." (He omitted to mention that there had been no direct appeal for aid from Jerusalem itself.) ". . . fight now against the Unbelievers, you who are wont to wage private wars . . ." He appealed for an end to fratricidal strife in Europe, and under the Truce of God pointed the way towards a common foe.

Upon his undernourished, ignorant, superstitious and mostly unprivileged audience, the effect was cataclysmal. Great shouts of *"Le Dieu le volt"* — "God wills it" — rent the air, and were taken up as the crowd dispersed, accompanied by itinerant preachers who were to keep the flames of enthusiasm and emotion fanned to fever pitch. Like wildfire the message raced abroad, and soon a great body, unorganized and un-disciplined, streamed across Europe, plundering to survive, only to be slaughtered at last by the Turks on the southern shores of the Bosphorus. Byzantium, elegant and cultured, was appalled by the spectacle of the ill-fated horde.

Behind them trod, with measured step, the barons and their armies. These fighting men came bound by feudal loyalties and with simple burning faith. Like some of those who had hurled themselves into the disastrous so-called "Peoples' Crusade", many had mortgaged their meagre smallholdings to the monasteries and churches in order to arm themselves and to buy food for the families they left behind. In simple faith, their wives had sewn the emblem of their Saviour's Cross upon their tunics, and had bidden them God speed upon the journey, of whose length and of whose hazards they had no conception. Accoutred each according to his rank, they set out upon their venture, full knowing that many marched forth never to return. Some were moved by ideals alone; others enlisted in search of booty and excitement, some to avoid retribution for crimes, and some to sever tedious or untenable domesticities. But their faith was strong, and absolution promised; for theirs was the Kingdom of Heaven.

They marched under leaders whose names and bravery the passing of time has made glorious. On through 1096, 1097 and 1098, years of hard campaigning against the elements and a courageous enemy, we pick up the campaign again after Baldwin of Boulogne had left the march to found the County of Edessa, Bohemond of Taranto to found the Principality of Antioch, and Raymond of Toulouse, the Principality of Tripoli.

Coptic patriarch's pectoral cross.

The vaulted ceiling of the Coptic Chapel of the Four Bodiless Heavenly Creatures (Deir El-Sultan).

These states were politically and commercially more important to the Franks than was Palestine. Only those whose motives were truly religious pressed on southwards.

On 7th June 1099 the pounding army had climbed up from the coastal plain, and breasted the ridge of hills above Emmaus. They then moved forward on their final tactical approach, and encamped before the walls of Jerusalem that night. Tancred, brother of Bohemond I of Taranto, and Baldwin of Bourg detached themselves with their mounted troops, swept round the right flank to the south, and secured Bethlehem and the southern approaches to the city. They rejoined the main force later before the walls and took post with Godfrey of Bouillon on the western sector below the Jaffa Gate. Robert of Normandy, the brother of William of England, commanded the northern sector from Herod's Gate to the north-east corner. Robert of Flanders held his right flank from the Damascus Gate to the north-west corner where Herod's Tower of Psephinus had stood. Godfrey of Lorraine was stationed from his right flank to the Jaffa Gate. In the south Raymond of Toulouse closed in on Mount Zion. The east side, rising steeply up from the Kidron Valley, was unopposed, as attack there presented insuperable problems. Whether the leaders knew it or not, the deployment of the army was similar to that adopted by Titus in A.D. 70. It was an ill omen for the small Fatimid garrison, which had expelled the unwanted Christian community before setting their defence in order.

The siege began on the night of the arrival, 7th June. It soon became clear that it could not be sustained for any length of time. The wells outside the city had been blocked or poisoned, and the armoured Crusaders were ill-suited to exert themselves in the hot Judean summer. After a series of abortive attacks, thirst, aggravated to an almost unbearable level by a hot dry Khamsin wind, skirmishing attacks by the defenders and by marauding bands of Muslim soldiers, together with acrimonious political arguments amongst the leaders, all helped to lower their morale. A decision, one way or the other, had to be achieved swiftly.

A fast was proclaimed on 5th July, lasting three days. Afterwards the army marched in procession, barefoot, round the city, taunted and jeered at by its defenders. Then they ascended the Mount of Olives, from which traditional vantage point pilgrims first prayed before the Holy City. Here the troops were subjected to stirring sermons and exhortations by their leaders. Morale recovered, and they were set to complete two huge siege towers and a third somewhat smaller. The attack was launched on the night of 13th July and the walls were breached by Godfrey's troops about midday on the 15th. The Damascus Gate was opened and the invaders poured in to commence a slaughter which lasted all afternoon, all evening, and the next day. Hundreds of Muslims who had taken refuge in the Aqsa Mosque were killed. Not a man, woman or child survived except the small garrison of the citadel, which surrendered after guaranteeing a huge ransom to Raymond of Toulouse. Raymond of Aguilers described how, in order to reach the Dome of the Rock, he had to pick his way through corpses and blood that reached up to his knees. The small Jewish community barricaded themselves into their synagogue and were all burnt with it. When there was no one left alive, the Crusaders took off their blood-soaked armour and walked barefoot to give thanks to God in the church which Constantine Monomachus had restored.

An Eastern Orthodox (Greek) archbishop.

Chapel of Abraham: doorway of the Iconastasis.

Soon after, Godfrey of Bouillon was elected King, following much acrimonious argument and manoeuvring. A man of greater piety than administrative ability, he refused the crown, and is sometimes quoted as saying: "How can I accept a crown of gold in the place where my Saviour was crowned with thorns?" He adopted the title of "Advocatus Sancti Sepulchri".

Arnulf of Rohes was appointed Patriarch, and the "Latinization" of the See of Jerusalem commenced. Twenty new Latin canons were appointed to the Church of the Resurrection, and all the Orthodox priests banished. The most important relics, including the pieces of the True Cross, had been taken for safety out of the city before the siege, and these were now recovered from their Orthodox guardians.

If it may appear that too much space has been given to the formation of the Crusader Kingdom, then it must be considered in its wider context. The Kingdom lasted for nearly two hundred years, with Jerusalem occupied for just half that time. But the effects upon history of this attempt to superimpose a western European presence and control over the Levantine crossroads of trade, politics and beliefs, between Asia and Africa and the south-eastern approaches to Europe, have been lasting. The basic European conditioning to the idea that the religion and the culture of the Arab-speaking world are inferior to its own, acquired at this time, has been as damaging as it has been erroneous, and we are still enmeshed in its coils.

Jerusalem of the Franks (1099 to 1187)

The news of the capture of Jerusalem was rapturously received in the countries of the Crusaders, many of whom now returned home, their pious duty well concluded. Pilgrims and settlers poured into Palestine and the business of colonization prospered, as fraternization leading to integration developed once the battle was done. Fulk of Chartres wrote in 1124, "For we who were western have now become eastern. Who was Roman or Frank has in this land become Galilaean or Palestinian. Already we have forgotten our native land . . . who there was poor, here God makes wealthy." Although this oversimplifies a hard life where drought and disease were constant threats, there is no doubt that part of the drive and initiative which had carried the newcomers from so far away was now canalized into the development of the land. Pilgrimage became a major element in the economy, especially for Jerusalem, which was cut off from the fertile coastal districts and the mercantile towns. But the earlier growing interchange of culture and technology between Byzantium and the Islamic States had been ruined, and the brutality of the Latin incursion ensured that when, in time, the land reverted to Muslim sovereignty, Christendom would never recover the status which it had formerly enjoyed as representing one of the "Peoples of the Book".

With the consolidation of their conquest of Palestine in progress, and the feudal organization for the administration of the land being imposed upon its peoples, we must return to the confines of the Church of the Resurrection and its welfare.

According to Michael of Syria, the Crusaders had vowed that if they were successful in capturing Jerusalem they would "live in peace with Christians of all confessions,

Sword and spurs of Godfrey de Bouillon.

The restored Crusader dome above the Katholicon.

and would give churches to every nation which confessed Christ." It is clear from this, at any rate, that all churches would belong to them, irrespective of previous possessors. In 1131 the work of restoration of the Church of the Resurrection began under total Latin direction and supervision. It was consecrated on 15th July 1149. This is substantially the building which we see today.

The builders were faced, initially, with the somewhat hasty and improvised repair work previously carried out, together with the expanse of Constantine's ruined Martyrion. Some of the columns and much of the fallen masonry had already been removed for use in building elsewhere. Obviously, the greatly increased Christian community needed a larger building than that which was available. The great achievement and the great difference from the preceding churches was the design by which all the Holy Places were incorporated under one roof. The east sector of the Rotunda (Anastasis) with its triforal doors was cut away and replaced by a great archway. This was connected to a Katholicon which stood over the former Atrium. The underground Chapel of Saint Helena was constructed with a broad staircase rising from the centre and turning left to admit to the southern transept. The Chapel of the Invention (Finding) of the Cross was repaired and decorated with mural frescoes on plaster over its rough-hewn walls. The three oratories which commemorated Saint Longinus, The Division of Christ's Raiment, and the Chapel of Insults became small chapels set into the ambulatory wall running behind the High Altar at the eastern end of the Katholicon. Calvary was built up with internal access (instead of by the flight of stairs from outside the south wall), with a vaulted ceiling. A doorway, on the north side, approached by a flight of steep steps, gave on to the street from the Chapel of Saint Mary the Virgin beside the Crusaders' Patriarchal Palace.

The main entrance was transferred to the south side, where two great doors were let into the walls. A belfry, three-tiered and domed, was built above the Chapel of the Forty Martyrs, and a cone-like dome with a large open centre was set upon the Rotunda. The Tomb itself would appear to have been a plain rectangular building surmounted by a small canopied aedicule. In a sense, the Rotunda formed the nave and the Katholicon the choir of a cathedral church. The colonnade on the north side became an aisle, or transept, and the southern transept enclosed the new constructions of Calvary and the Adam Chapel. The eastern part of the new church was thus set almost entirely upon the west base-line of Constantine's Martyrion. The floor of the Martyrion became part of the cloisters of Saint Mary of the Latins, and a small cupola with windows was inserted in order to let light into the Chapel of Saint Helena below. The new Atrium (or Parvis) on the south side may well have been connected with Hardian's forum. Be that as it may, in Crusader times it was set over a vaulted cistern, and approached through an arched portico, the remains of which can be seen today beside the street.

In 1131 Fulk of Anjou was crowned in the Church of the Resurrection instead of at Bethlehem as was the custom previously. Subsequent kings followed suit, in a ceremony which involved the exchanging of oaths affirming mutual support and defence between King and Patriarch.

While the reconstruction of the church proceeded, the Turks were once more moving south and putting pressure upon the Latin Kingdom. Necessity demanded a united

Jewelled crystal case of the Crusaders, containing relics of saints. Mounted upon a spear shaft, it was carried in procession or into battle.

The dome above the Katholicon seen from the north transept (Arches of the Virgin).

Christian front. Although this was achieved in theory, in practice Byzantine mistrust for previous Frankish deception and deceit was cordially reciprocated. But faced with the common threat, both Muslims and Christians in Palestine entered a period of accord and amicability.

An abortive Second Crusade, following the fall of Edessa in 1144, served to stiffen Muslim resolve to recover their lost lands and avenge their defeats. On the other hand, failure by the Franks to appreciate the military necessity for dominating communications was a fatal mistake, and the continuing Arab occupation of the towns, except for Jerusalem and the coastal ports, further weakened control over internal security.

1171 saw the Fatimid Caliphate pass to the great Ayyubite Salah al-Din. By 1174, following the death of the Atabeg Nur ed-Din in Damascus, Salah al-Din, or Saladin as he was called in the West, took over the crown of Syria as well as that of Egypt. The Crusader King Almaric had died that same year, and while the Muslims consolidated a united front, the Frankish Kingdom was weakened by sickly kings and scheming nobles. The end was inevitable, but it was precipitated by the treacherous behaviour of Reynald of Chatillon, Lord of Kerak.

On Friday 3rd July 1187, the army of the Crusaders were tempted out from behind their defences to fight under adverse conditions at Hattin, near Tiberias. Bad generalship and tactics could not be mitigated by the bravery of exhausted, thirst-crazed soldiers. King Guy was captured and ransomed, the military knights, who neither gave nor expected any quarter in battle, were executed to a man, and the True Cross was taken in triumph to Damascus. Quickly cutting off the ports to prevent the arrival of sea-borne reinforcements, Salah al-Din rode into Jerusalem on 2nd October 1187.

Lead seal of King Baldwin of Jerusalem.

The Second Muslim Period (1187 to 1517)

Salah al-Din's treatment of the Holy City was in strict accordance with Muslim veneration for Jesus and for his teaching. It was in marked contrast to the investment of Jerusalem by the Crusaders a hundred years earlier.

The garrison was allowed to ransom itself, most modestly. Many who could not pay were given free passage. All Franks were escorted to the coast and put into Genoese and Venetian ships. The Gold Cross that had been placed upon the Dome of the Rock was removed, and the Rock itself was cleansed with rosewater after having carried an altar upon it during its years as a Christian Cathedral ("Templum Domini"). The Aqsa Mosque was restored to its proper purpose (the Knights Templar had used it as their headquarters), and the Church of the Resurrection was safeguarded and returned to the care of the Orthodox Church. Salah al-Din forbade pilgrimage, but, by virtue of the military success of the Third Crusade in 1192, Richard I of England (Coeur de Lion) negotiated with Salah al-Din a treaty by which pilgrimage was resumed, and some Latin priests were allowed to return to Jerusalem. It is worth recording that at this time the Muslim Nuseibah family were given custody of the keys to the Church of the Holy Sepulchre, as part of the measures taken to prevent disputes between Christian factions: an office still held by the family today.

The Armenian Chapel of Saint Helena

The Third Crusade came to an end with the signing of Richard's treaty. He set sail from Palestine, leaving a smaller but temporarily secure kingdom which stretched along the coast from Tyre to Jaffa, with access only under sufferance to its titular capital, Jerusalem.

Salah al-Din died in 1193. Truly it is said of him that he fulfilled every requirement and virtue sought and cherished by his greatest enemies, the Christian Knights. He is buried in Damascus, but his decorative work and restorations to the Dome of the Rock, to the Aqsa Mosque, and elsewhere in Jerusalem, are fitting memorials to a leader who feared God, fought hard and ruled justly.

At the beginning of the thirteenth century a new intervention, this time by Germans, had some far-reaching effects arising out of a brief stay in the Holy Land. Frederick II, Emperor of Germany, had vowed under papal duress to undertake a Crusade, but he postponed his departure year by year. Instead he started to negotiate with the Arabs from his base in Sicily, where he had acquired a knowledge of Arabic and the ways of the Levant from his Mediterranean subjects and from Arab scholars. His pacific attitude further angered the Pope, who insisted that Jerusalem must be retaken by force of arms and that none should treat with "infidels". Frederick was excommunicated and was thus finally obliged to undertake his procrastinated campaign. However, on arrival in Acre in 1228, he still managed to avoid military activity. To the embarrassment of the Pope, he successfully concluded a treaty with the Malik al-Kamil. This, by peaceful means, achieved more than anyone could have hoped. To Frederick were conceded Jerusalem, Bethlehem, Nazareth and Western Galilee, together with a corridor from the Holy City to Jaffa seaport. In return, he was obliged to keep Jerusalem unfortified and to leave the Dome of the Rock and Al-Aqsa Mosque in Muslim possession; no undue hardship with which to comply in order to secure such concessions.

As a further insult to the Pope, Frederick had himself crowned in the Church of the Resurrection in 1229, opposed by the outraged clergy and the Frankish chivalry, and supported only by his own troops and the Teutonic Knights, who had now greatly increased their numbers. Regrettably, he was forced to leave Jerusalem soon after, and the situation rapidly deteriorated. Frederick was a man of true courage and some humour, as well as being a deft and skilful diplomat.

Vacillating policies ensued. A treaty made by the Franks with Syria against Egypt caused a savage attack by Khwarzimian (Turkish) mercenaries, who devastated Syria and Palestine and sacked Jerusalem in 1244. All Christian priests who were in the city were killed and the churches were once more desecrated. Thousands of citizens who had been given leave to flee to Jaffa were ambushed and slaughtered. The city was finally abandoned and the rump of the kingdom dragged on, under merciless attack from the Mamelukes under Baybars al-Bandukdari. At last, in May 1291, Acre fell, soon followed by the rearguard at Athlit. The Crusader Kingdom in Palestine had ended, one hundred and fifty-six years after Pope Urban II had appealed for its creation. But the Crusades were not yet over, nor indeed would they ever leave the minds of Christian men. In defensive warfare from Cyprus, Rhodes and Malta, the knights fought on against the Ottoman Turks, who were finally to carry their banners as far

Cross of Lorraine, carved in the south doorway of the Church.

Chapel of Abraham: a multiple lamp-holder.

as the walls of Vienna in 1529 under the command of Suleiman, known as "The Magnificent".

In other fields, the concept of the Crusades lived on. With the sign of the Cross upon their sails the European navigators and explorers set forth upon their voyages to discover lands, peoples, and riches as yet unknown. "In this sign you shall conquer": thus they followed in the steps of Constantine.

The Mamelukes now had control of the whole country. They succeeded, remarkably, in repelling the Mongol hordes, keeping them out of Palestine. Pilgrimage diminished, and by 1382 Jews and Christians were barred from public office and forced to wear yellow and blue turbans respectively. Political harassment and military activities by Christian powers abroad had an uncomfortable habit of bringing down recrimination upon the head of the dwindling Christian population of Jerusalem. At one time, there were only two or three monks in the whole city. Regulations such as a ban on riding horses (mules were permitted) were strictly enforced. Marriage or cohabitation with Muslims was punishable by death; church bells were forbidden to be rung, and many churches were themselves destroyed, or turned into mosques or secular buildings.

As always, political considerations ameliorated the situation from time to time. The Georgians, ferocious fighters from the northern Caucasus, manoeuvred themselves into a prime position in the Church of the Resurrection, becoming sole custodians of Calvary, the chapels of Saint Helena and of the Invention (Finding) of the Cross, and the Prison of Christ.

They also took over the Monastery of The Cross, west of the city. Similarly, the Ethiopians, whose country lay on the southern border of Egypt, exercised considerable influence. For example, a threat to destroy all mosques and Muslims in Ethiopia neutralized a move by the Mamelukes to destroy the Holy Places; itself a reaction to a threat of a new Crusade preached by Pope Eugene in 1344.

Such other authority as could be obtained from the sultans tended to go to the Orthodox clergy, possibly because of natural preference by the Muslims for any Christian rather than a Latin, but probably, on a more practical level, as their "rewards" were larger. However, by 1400, records show that all the major churches were represented again: Armenians, Copts, Syrians and Ethiopians, with the Latin Church represented by Franciscans. Palm Sunday processions were allowed, and the capitation fee was removed from entry into the Church of the Resurrection. None the less it was a bleak period for Christendom.

The Third Muslim (Ottoman) Period (1517 to 1917)

The Ottoman Turks finally took over Palestine and Egypt in 1517. A reforming start after the ruinous end to Mameluke rule soon gave way to indolence, and the country lapsed into apathy under corrupt officials and self-indulgent sultans. Heavy taxation and bribery were the characteristics of government once Suleiman the Magnificent was

Panel of an Orthodox episcopal chasuble (Saint Catherine).

Eastern Orthodox Chapel of Saint John.

dead (1566). He had built much, including the present walls, and improved the facilities of Jerusalem.

The churches, on the other hand, pursued the course of reinstatement with vigour. In 1535 France and the Sublime Porte (Constantinople) concluded an agreement, called the Capitulations, giving France a coastal trade monopoly, and the Franciscans returned to the Church of the Resurrection. In 1555, they were able to carry out extensive and long overdue repairs, including a new aedicule above the Sepulchre. The Capitulations contained seventeen articles in all, and gave to France the role of protector of the Catholics in Palestine. The Franciscans, however, were dislodged from Mount Zion by the Muslims and took up their residence in the monastery of Saint Saviour, which remains their headquarters today. They also gained rights in Bethlehem. Further French diplomatic activity in 1604 resulted in the guarantee of Muslim protection of the Christian Holy Places, as well as of those who visited them. The Turks were happy to encourage pilgrimage, which brought in much-needed revenue. By bringing the Latin and Orthodox Churches into proximity and some balance they could enjoy a rivalry which would also prove financially rewarding to them. Protestant pilgrims started to appear in Jerusalem at this time. Jews began to return to Palestine in some numbers. Some started schools of messianic expectation and mysticism in Galilee, while others returned to Jerusalem to devote themselves to religious study. These people, most of them refugees from Russian and European persecution, had neither wealth nor much opportunity, even if they had the desire, to earn their living. They were dependent upon charitable donations from Jewish communities abroad, collected by travelling emissaries, which system was to become the basis of Zionist fund-raising in later years.

Orthodox icon set in a bishop's throne in the Katholicon.

The Capitulations do not seem to have affected the granting of "hatti-sherif" or "firmans" (licences), quite independently, by the Sublime Porte. In 1605, although the French and their Latin protégés were under "most favoured nation" terms, the Orthodox Christians were granted possession of the Place of Crucifixion, which has remained in their custody. In 1637, the Orthodox further acquired the Church of the Nativity with its gardens in Bethlehem, and the Holy Sepulchre itself, the Stone of Unction or Anointment, and the remainder of Calvary. This firman was confirmed in 1675.

Earlier, in 1664, the Georgians were evicted from the Church of the Resurrection because they could not pay their dues, and four years later the Ethiopians suffered a similar fate. The Coptic representation was reduced to one priest by 1698.

International politics, in the form of French support of the Turks against military pressures from Venice, Austria and Poland, enabled the balance in favour of the Orthodox to be swung back towards the Latins. The firman of 1690 gave the Latin (or Catholic) Church superiority in the Church of the Resurrection, the Sepulchre itself, both domes, the Unction Stone, the Arches of the Virgin (north transept) and the southern half of Calvary. In Bethlehem, they regained the Grotto of the Nativity, the Basilica and its gardens.

The state of the Dome over the Anastasis (Rotunda) had seriously deteriorated, as had the belfry adjacent. Permission was given to the Latins to repair the Dome in 1719 and

The eastern apse and dome above the Katholicon. In the foreground, Ethiopian cells stand upon the floor of Constantine's former Matyrion.

to the Orthodox to reduce the height of the bell tower at the same time. An opening 30 feet wide in the top of the Dome was insisted upon; this was covered with wire netting.

A successful diplomatic intervention by France on Turkey's behalf again, this time against Austria and Russia, enabled France to sign new Capitulations with her weakened partner in 1740. The firman of 1690 was confirmed and, most important, it bound not only the signatories but their successors. Moreover, it clearly "expressed concern" for the safety of the Franciscans. This all-embracing phrase was to be of the utmost use in defending encroachment upon Latin rights at later dates, and, since the document was technically an international treaty, no change or alteration affecting it could legally be made without the consent of France.

Following an outbreak of violence when the Orthodox community attacked the Franciscans in Holy Week 1757, a firman was issued restoring the Orthodox to their positions of 1675. In addition, the Latins were ejected from the Tomb of the Virgin Mary in Gethsemane by the Orthodox. This firman established what has become known as the Status Quo, and set out in great detail the rights enjoyed by each community.*

On 11th October 1808, a fire, which had started in an Armenian chapel, swept through the Church, bringing down the Dome of the Anastasis and doing immense damage throughout the building, especially to the aedicule about the Tomb. The flames that were eventually extinguished did not include the fires of fanaticism, which continued to rage. Latins and Orthodox sought to obtain exclusive permission to carry out the repairs, thereby adding to or further securing their areas of control and custodianship. Eventually, the Orthodox were successful in obtaining permission to carry out the necessary repairs, partly because Europe was immersed in the Napoleonic Wars and had little time to spare for events in Jerusalem.

The repairs, carried out somewhat hurriedly within two years, incorporated some added advantage to the Orthodox, which was to be expected. New doors were fitted in the entrance, and the apse was virtually rebuilt. The majority of the columns of the Anastasis had been considerably damaged and weakened, and now all were encased in plaster pillars. The ambulatory was divided up by small cells. A new Unction Stone was set and walls were erected down the insides of the transepts, cutting them off from the Katholicon. The Coptic Chapel was added to the western end of the aedicule of the Sepulchre. During repairs to Calvary the opportunity was taken to obliterate the tombs of Baldwin I, Godfrey of Bouillon, and a third Crusader King who may have been Baldwin II or Fulk of Anjou. The tomb of Philip d'Aubigny, who had come to Jerusalem with Frederick II in 1228, was not disturbed since it lay at that time beneath a stone seat for the Muslim doorkeepers. Three smaller arches were built to support the great arch between the Anastasis and the Katholicon.

In 1834, such was the crush and excitement engendered by the Ceremony of the Holy Fire that panic ensued and hundreds of worshippers and pilgrims were trampled to death, threatening once more the structure of the Church. In 1836, the Dome over the

* See *The Status Quo in the Holy Places*, L. G. A. Cust, HMSO, 1929.

Illuminated Armenian gospel of Thoros Roslin (1265) showing Saint Luke.

Armenian patriarchal belt with a pearl set in a triangular gold buckle. The sides of the triangle are 12 centimetres.

Anastasis was in danger of collapse again, and the work of repairing it was carried out for the first time at the shared expense of Turkey, Russia and France. 1841 saw the creation of the Anglican bishopric, and six years later the Latin Patriarchate was re-established in 1847, after a period of four hundred years of inactivity.

Russia had by now taken over responsibility as Protecting Power of the Orthodox Church, and kept pressing for further curtailment of Latin privileges. In 1852 Russia went so far as to claim authority over all people of the Orthodox faith anywhere in the Ottoman Empire. Turkey considered this to be an attempt to usurp its sovereignty, and Russia went to war with Turkey, ostensibly to impose her demands, but equally to try to establish herself south of the Black Sea, in the warm waters of the Mediterranean, an age-old dream. Turkey appealed to England and France, who, whatever they may or may not have felt about the welfare of Orthodox Christians in the Ottoman Empire, were quite clear and united in their desire to keep Russia out of the Mediterranean. Thus began the Crimean War in 1855. At its conclusion three years later, the provisions of the existing firman were confirmed. In return for French and English support and the pressure from increased international concern for the Holy City, some notional rights of equality were granted to non-Muslims in the Ottoman Empire. By an Edict of Toleration in 1856, all religions were officially recognized within the empire, non-Muslims having been readmitted to the Haram Al-Sharif in the previous year.

In 1852, preceding the outbreak of the Crimean War, a firman had been issued setting out the divisions of the Holy Places under the Status Quo. Reaffirmed later by the Treaty of Berlin in 1878, it is this firman which stands today.*

The opening of the Suez Canal in 1869 added to the strategic importance of Palestine, and therefore attracted further attention and concern by the European powers. The take-over of Egypt by Britain in 1882 brought the British into direct confrontation with the Muslims of Palestine for the first time since the knights had sailed away in 1251. Foreign consulates became numerous. Missionary, educational and welfare work developed rapidly. 1864 had seen the beginning of a complete survey of Palestine and, reflecting the revival of general and academic interest in the Holy Land, the Palestine Exploration Fund was set up in London in the following year.

In 1885 the Orthodox Patriarchate assigned certain rights to the Anglican Church which enabled it to hold occasional services in the Chapel of Abraham on the south side of the Church of the Resurrection. The right is always granted when so requested, because it is clearly understood by all parties that the Anglican Church lays no claim to any of the Holy Places.

In 1898 Kaiser Wilhelm II paid a visit to Jerusalem as part of Germany's campaign to wean Turkey away from her European allies, France and Britain, and to impose German

Armenian illuminated gospel of Thoros Roslin (1256) showing Saint Matthew.

* "As a result of the Commission's researches and the deliberations in his Cabinet Council, the Sultan issued in February 1852 the final firman on the Holy Places 'to serve constantly and for ever as permanent rule'. The firman defines the places in dispute, investigates the conflicting claims, pronounces a blessing over Jesus and the Virgin Mary whenever their names are mentioned, and decides on the main issue 'that all these places must be left in their present state.' It therefore confirmed in essence the status which had existed since 1757." From *Israel and the Holy Places of Christendom*, by Walter Zander, Weidenfeld and Nicolson, 1971.

The Coptic Chapel set in the western end of the aedicule of the Sepulchre.

influence upon the important trade route to the East. At this time, the Lutherans built their fine Church of the Redeemer upon or adjacent to the site of Saint Mary of the Latins, and were also given extensive grants of land both in Jerusalem and elsewhere in Palestine.

The Anglican Cathedral Church of Saint George was built to the north of the city, on the Nablus Road beyond the Dominican convent of Saint Stephen. With the growth of Christian pilgrimage, residential settlements grew up outside the city, the first of which was built by Moses Montefiore for Jews. Naturally, the Greek, Armenian and Catholic Churches expanded, and filled their quarters inside the Old City around the Mother Church.

World War I broke out in 1914, and Turkey allied herself with Germany. At the end of June 1917, General Sir Edmund Allenby opened a campaign with British and Arab forces. Having marched from Egypt, he reached Jerusalem in December, and on 11th December he made his formal entry into the city through the Jaffa Gate. The inhabitants remembered an old saying: "When the Nile overflows into Palestine, Al-Nebi (the prophet) from the West will drive the Turk from Jerusalem."

Apart from the military campaign, which ended with the Commander-in-Chief reaffirming the Status Quo of the Holy Places, the most far-reaching event of the war so far as Jerusalem was concerned was the publication of the British letter, dated 2nd November 1917, known as the Balfour Declaration. While this agreed in principle to the establishment of a Jewish national home in Palestine, it provided clear safeguards regarding the civil and religious rights of the existing non-Jewish communities. Its loose wording was probably so intended in order that interpretation could be as flexible as possible; that it should be "all things to all men" at a period of extreme precariousness for Britain in the war. It did, however, specifically state "that nothing shall be done which may prejudice the civil and religious rights of existing non-Jewish communities in Palestine."

Armenian illuminated gospel of Thoros Roslin (1256) showing Saint Mark.

The Mandate Period (1920 to 1948)

In 1920 Britain took over the Mandate for Palestine on behalf of the League of Nations. This was in direct contradiction of promises of independence made by the Allies to the Arabs in exchange for their participation in the war against the Turks.

Seven years later, a severe earthquake rocked Jerusalem, and much serious damage was done. A structural survey also revealed that the Dome above the Rotunda should have been brought down for safety reasons, due to the deterioration of the mortar used in the twelfth-century building. Subsidence and buckling were taking place, caused principally by the immense weight of the two domes and the roof. The foundations were, for the most part, sound. As no agreement could be reached between the religious communities for sharing the repair work, the Mandate Government was obliged to step in and erect massive ironwork scaffolding and buttresses in order to prevent the total collapse of the Church.

From now until the end of the Mandate, the British were subjected to attack by both

The Eastern Orthodox Chapel of Abraham.

Jews and Muslims. In November 1947, the United Nations Organization, without permitting the population of Palestine to exercise its right of self-determination as a colonial people under the United Nations Charter, agreed to divide the country between the two disputants, with the city of Jerusalem and the Holy Places about it, including Bethlehem, as a separate and international enclave. This was unacceptable to both sides, and, as the United Nations Organization was unable to impose its plan, battle was once more joined for possession of Palestine and the Holy Places.

The Post-Mandate Period (1948 onwards)

At the termination of the Mandate in 1948, the state of Israel was proclaimed by the Jews, and a new Diaspora was created, this time composed of Muslims and Christians, who fled from Jewish attack into neighbouring Lebanon, Jordan and elsewhere. The Old City of Jerusalem and what was left of Palestine were incorporated into the Hashemite Kingdom of Jordan in 1952.

The urgent work of reconstruction of the Church of the Resurrection eventually began in 1952, and was given additional impetus by the visit of Pope Paul VI to Jordan and Israel in 1964, and by his meeting with the Patriarchs of the Eastern Churches. With further advances made at the great Ecumenical Council in the Vatican, a plan for complete restoration and repair was agreed upon and finally put into effect. A joint architectural advisory committee was formed and an office established at the southern side of the Parvis in the Orthodox Monastery of Gethsemane. From here the work has been carried forward step by step. The removal of the nineteenth century walls which cut off the Katholicon from the transepts literally and metaphorically opened up the entire structure, to the joy of all who behold it. As the work proceeds, confidence is gained, disputed areas are narrowed down, and agreements are reached for the general benefit. The stripping away of the plastering, not only in the Anastasis but all over the church, has removed much of the darkness, and the slow but steady removal of the scaffolding put up in 1927 has exposed once more the strong, elegant masonry.

A significant ecumenical event took place in October 1965, when the miraculously preserved body of Saint Savvas (Mar Saba, referred to earlier) returned to Jerusalem. He had founded his famous Lavra (convent) in 491 and was buried there after his death in 533. At the time of the Crusades he had been removed to Venice, where he had remained within the Latin Church of Saint Mark. During the course of His Holiness Pope Paul VI's visit to Jerusalem, the Orthodox Patriarch Benedictus petitioned His Holiness for the return of the most Venerated Relics of the Saint, to which the Pope acceded.

Clad once more in the robes of the Eastern Orthodox Church, Saint Savvas travelled back to Jerusalem, to lie in state before returning in 1966 once more to the tomb in which his body had first rested 1,433 years previously.

In 1967, renewed hostilities broke out between Israel and Jordan. Thousands of new refugees streamed across the River Jordan to swell the ranks of those displaced nine years previously. The remainder of Palestine, and with it the Church of the Resurrection,

Seal of King Baldwin of Jerusalem (reverse).

Restored rib-vaulting of the Crusader Church above the Katholicon and eastern apse.

was captured by the Israelis, and the Old City of Jerusalem with its environs was assimilated by Israeli law into the State of Israel.

The Church Today (1974)

Thus does the ancient city stand, phoenix-like upon the ashes of each conqueror's temporal — and temporary — triumph.

From the corners of the world, the pilgrims stream into Jerusalem. However brief their visit to this Mother Church of Christianity may be, none can escape the sense of history that pervades its atmosphere. For many, the reality does not match their preconceptions. But upon all, the effect of their confrontation with the place of the Crucifixion and of the Risen Christ is positive. Even the tangled web of architecture and the interwoven pattern of the different offices and services cannot detract from the power of the central theme of Jesus' exemplary defiance of the shackles by which mankind is bound.

For those more fortunate, able to return daily or at intervals of time, the sounds and shapes of apparent discord eventually harmonize and become understood; the jigsaw turns into mosaic, and seemingly contradictory voices blend into complicated but nevertheless comprehensive euphony.

On approaching the Church across the Crusaders' Parvis, stop and look. To the left you will see the Chapel of Saint James, the Parish Church of the Arab Orthodox Community, the Chapel of Saint John, and that of the Forty Martyrs with the Belfry over it; on the right stands the Orthodox convent of Saint Abraham with the vast cistern of Saint Helena beneath it, the chapels of Saint John, Saint Michael and the inaccessible Saint Mary of Egypt.

Beneath the Parvis, the arched vaults rest upon re-used Hadrianic columns, and we stand upon the bedrock of the hillside of Golgotha itself. At its northern extremity may be seen the single span of the Crusaders' arch which supports the double entrance-way. In the dampness and discolorations of the rock, traces of the red earth can still be found, indicative of the "garden" which was set about the ancient tombs outside the city wall.

Back upon the Parvis, we stand beside the masons, chipping and cutting with dusty skill. Apart from the surveying of the foundations and the upper structure, a force of craftsmen was assembled to replace marble that had "died", and to carve replicas of columns and capitals that had been eroded by time. The chipping of their mallets sounded like orchestral timpani, and fine white dust-clouds swirled about the Church and the surrounding buildings, like incense sanctifying the activity of re-creation. Slowly the new pieces were slotted into place, some capitals were marked, drawn and carved *in situ*. In many instances, the old designs were faithfully redrawn, but occasionally the masons gave contemporary expression to their craft, and, as is their wont, did not exclude discreet humour.

Amongst the scaffolding, lifting-tackle and the massive blocks, pilgrims and priests threaded their way, diverted but not deflected from the order of their devotions. The

Icon of Saint James in the Orthodox Chapel of the Saint.

This view of the Katholicon was taken before the Iconastasis was replaced. It shows the Crusader choir in its entirety with the "Centre of the World" in the foreground.

impedimenta of reconstruction dwindle. The new stone, which comes from the same quarries of Kalandia, north of the city, that supplied the material for the twelfth-century church and for that of Constantine, begins to blend in with the old; worked and set by hands of masons whose forefathers created that amongst which it now takes its place.

In front rises the façade. The scaffolding has now been removed, and we can see the superb romanesque decoration of the twelfth century. Worth noting especially are the indented or bevelled gadroons about the windows. These, though popular with Arab designers, were never much used in the West. Of the twin doors, the right-hand one has been closed since the time of Salah al-Din. From above both doors, the lintels, which show biblical scenes carved in bas-relief, have been removed for safety to the Palestinian Archaeological Museum. A grille in the pavement covers Sir Philip D'Aubigny's tomb, referred to previously. In the right-hand corner, twelve steps lead up to the little Chapel of the Franks, or Our Lady of Sorrows. It used to be a small external atrium and entrance to Calvary but is not so used now as there are internal stairs. Beneath it lies the Chapel of Saint Mary of Egypt.

Entering by the left-hand doorway, and paying our respects to the doorkeepers, we must turn right immediately (resisting temptation to proceed further), for only by so doing can we keep clear the relationships between history and topography. The stairway leads steeply up the hewn side of the hillock of Calvary until we stand upon its summit, 5 metres above the floor of the Church. It is divided into two chapels. On the right, beneath vaultings of sparkling modern (1937) Latin mosaics, is the Chapel of the Nailing to the Cross. In the middle still nestles the last fragment of the mediaeval decorations: Christ Ascending. Upon its walls, mosaic scenes depict Abraham's Sacrifice, the Mourning Women, and, behind the altar, the Mother stands in speechless shock beside the body of her lifeless Son. This altar was the gift of Ferdinand de Medici, Duke of Tuscany, in 1588.

Orthodox icon set in a bishop's throne in the Katholicon.

Between the two chapels is a small Franciscan altar dedicated to Our Lady of Sorrows, backed by a sculptured image of the Mater Dolorosa, encased, and hung about with priceless thank-offerings. The split rock of Calvary can be seen here where earthquake rent it. The Orthodox chapel on the north side is in typical and marked contrast. Its vaulted roof, dripping with lamps, is shadowed and mysterious. From its dark painted surface sensuous figures gleam amid exotic clouds. Here, behind a curtain of gold, silver and jewels, Christ stretches out his arms, in the paradoxical triumph of His Crucifixion. Beneath the altar, a silver-bordered space shows the traditional place into which the cross was set.

Coming down from Calvary into the south transept, we reach the Unction Stone, or Stone of Anointment. We are now back at ground level. The polished red granite covers the site of a former Oratory to Saint Mary Magdalene which marked the place where the body of Christ was prepared for burial. The lamps and candelabra above it are owned by the various communities in strict accordance with the Status Quo. Proceeding towards the Rotunda or Anastasis, we pass the wrought iron aedicule of the Armenians, which commemorates the three women who watched the historic tragedy enacted. It is about here, on a line drawn north – or across to our right – that Constantine's

Restoration work completed above the south transept

workmen cut through the hillside, leaving the Tomb freestanding where it can now be seen through the pillars and columns of the encircling Rotunda. (It is nearly 22 metres) from Calvary to the Tomb.) If we go straight ahead, passing behind the marble aedicule which now encloses the Tomb, and behind the ambulatory, we find ourselves back inside the rock with the quarried tombs, attributed to Saint Joseph of Arimathea, west of the Syrian Chapel. The presence of these tombs is a further conclusive indication that this area was outside the city at the time of the Crucifixion. Here, Christian Street is some 5 metres above our heads.

Turn back to the Rotunda, pausing a moment by the little Coptic Chapel, set in the western end of the Tomb's aedicule. Here immense work is going on to restore the building to its twelfth-century form. The plaster casements are being stripped away and some of the buried columns are revealed as being Constantinian. The lower courses of Constantine's Anastasis are visible in places, particularly behind the western side below Christian Street. Two galleries, the lower shared by the Latins and Armenians, and the upper belonging to the Orthodox, support the Dome. This, made of iron in 1868, replaced the wooden one which was destroyed by the fire of 1808. Now it too is badly in need of repair and re-decoration. The imposition of the massive pillars and the store-rooms reduced the diameter of the Rotunda from over 30 metres to just under 20 metres.

The aedicule surrounding the Tomb is of red marble, ornate and held together by iron stays. Sixteen pillars are built around its walls and it is surmounted by a Russian-style cupola. It is approximately 8·3 metres long and nearly 6 metres in height and width. A profusion of lamps hang before paintings of the Resurrection above the entrance to a vestibule or outer chamber. This is most ornately decorated. A fragment of the supposed stone which was rolled across the entrance is kept in a casket set on a marble pedestal. The Tomb itself is richly bedecked. A marble altar runs along the right-hand side above the shelf upon which Christ's body was placed. A cluster of lamps hang in claustrophobic splendour, gold and silver, in the amber baroque casement. It is not easy here to visualize a cold and misty dawn upon a hillside, with clumps of vegetation and olive trees about the gaping entrance to an empty tomb.

Leaving the Tomb behind, and passing under the archway facing its entrance, enter the Katholicon, which stands upon the Atrium of Constantine. Involution and complexity are here released from confinement and rise, as the eye follows the soaring perpendiculars, to become resolved in the rounded perfection of the Crusaders' Dome, itself saved from destruction and collapse. Beneath its apex stands the little Omphalos — "The Centre of the World". The floor is now being covered with polished marble. All around, with the nineteenth-century walls removed, the Iconastasis yet to be replaced before the Apse, the clean, renewed stone glows in the light which floods in from upper windows. Here Romanesque merges into early Gothic, and the false rib-vaulted ceiling bears witness to its English origin. Where possible, the original capitals and stones remain; where not, the modern copies are blended by the skill of masons who are themselves descendants of those who first carved the originals.

Retrace your steps beneath the great archway and turn right across the Rotunda. Beyond the north transept lies the Franciscan sacristy and the Church of the Appari-

Bevelled gadroons set above the twin doors of the south entrance to the Church.

Calvary: the Latin chapel on the right, Orthodox chapel on the left (north), with the shrine of Our Lady of Sorrows in between.

tion to Saint Mary. The former keeps the knightly relics, supposedly of Godfrey of Bouillon, and in the latter an altar is set about the stub of a pillar, claimed to be that upon which Christ was scourged. This conflicts directly with the Convent of the Flagellation, built over the ruins of Herod's Antonia Fortress at the beginning of the Pilgrims' Via Dolorosa. Be that as it may, it still commemorates a cruel practice, whose only merit was that by its very brutality it hastened merciful death to those subsequently crucified. Beyond this church, in the Franciscan Convent, one comes to a passage-way, which leads west, or left, to the old Crusader Patriarchate and refectory. Of note here is the stairway which rises sharply to a doorway. This gives out on to Christian Street at ground level, where it can be seen half destroyed and closed up. Part of the former Patriarchate is incorporated into the Khanqa Mosque nearby.

The altar of Saint Mary Magdalene stands at the western end of the north transept called the Arches of the Virgin. This is bounded by a profusion of pillars dating from Constantine Monomachus and later reinforced by others in the twelfth century, a discordant mixture of ineptly re-used fragments alongside shafts of Frankish elegance. We follow this transept round, past the Prison of Christ and the lonely chapels of Saint Longinus. The Division of Raiment, to the broad flight of steps which lead down to the Armenian Chapel of Saint Helena. Upon the walls, here and elsewhere, are serried rows of little crosses, carved by countless pilgrims throughout the centuries as mute reminders of their passage, an indelible prayer cut into the body of the Church. The surface of the stone is smooth with the patina of human touch, which traced its ageless surface in wonderment and mystery. The chapel was restored in 1950, but its massive stunted columns probably date from the seventh century. In its roof, the crusaders set a small cupola to bring in the light of day. Descending further still, we reach the Chapel of the Invention (Finding) of the Cross, now jointly held by the Latins and the Orthodox. Originally the Crypt below Constantine's Martyrion, its rough-hewn walls denote its former status as a cistern, and plastered remnants of Crusader frescoes have been discovered upon their surface; alas, too damaged for repair. The altar set on the left-hand side was the gift of the tragic Archduke Maximilian of Austria, who, as Emperor of Mexico, was assassinated in 1864.

Climbing up the stairway to the Ambulatory again, we pass the third chapel set behind the Apse, that of the Mocking of Christ. We can return to the south transept and the doorway, passing through the Chapel of Adam, beneath Calvary. Here two stone benches are all that indicates the tombs of the first Crusader Kings, Godfrey of Bouillon and Baldwin I. A third lies nearby. The legend of Christ's Crucifixion above the grave of Adam is lightly held, and no great concern is shown for the chapel which recalls it. Only a further glimpse of the split rock of Calvary is noteworthy.

Leaving the Church, turn left and out on to the street through the narrow entrance to the Parvis. The roads here are broad and stretch up through the Suk Aftimos — built to take Wilhelm II's carriage. Immediately on the right stands the Lutheran Church of the Redeemer upon the foundations of Saint Mary of the Latins. On the left, past the shops, lies the Russian Convent of Alexandros Nefki (the Russian Excavations). We have walked parallel to Constantine's Basilica and Atrium, and now turn left to enter it again. We have already plotted our position from the arches and masonry beneath the Russian

Armenian illuminated gospel of Thoros Roslin (1295) showing Saint John.

Altar of the Tomb of Christ.

Convent and the adjoining shop. We know that facing west we are standing where five steps led up from the Cardo Maximus to the Great Triple Archway and the colonnaded Atrium before Constantine's Basilica. We go forward up a slope which leads to the Coptic Convent. Before we reach it, however, a small doorway in the left opens on to a court which places us directly over the entrance to Constantine's Basilica.

Here, beneath friendly mulberry trees and dolorous, gentle peppers, the Ethiopians cling to their place by the Church, in a huddle of humble cells upon the floor of the long lost Martyrion. To the south the ruined wall of the Crusaders' Cloisters traces a telltale line of pointed masonry, upon which hangs apologetically a cluster of small bells. In the middle we see the cupola set in the roof of the Chapel of Saint Helena, and behind it the apse of the church, rebuilt in 1809, rising up to the twin domes above the roof. All the area forms the monastery of Deir el-Sultan, held by the Copts, but under counterclaim from the Ethiopians. Since 1967 the position of the Copts has been under great pressure, since pilgrimage from Egypt has halted, and political difficulties have increased. Nevertheless, they maintain their school and seminary adjacent to the Church of the Resurrection, and the custodianship of the Church of the Four Living Bodiless Creatures, the Chapel of Saint Michael and a great cistern, also dedicated to Saint Helena.

At the entrance to Deir el-Sultan is the Ninth Station of the Cross, marked by a column set into the wall. It is the last Station before the Via Dolorosa enters the Church of the Resurrection.

I hope that this brief tour will give not only a physical description but also some feeling for the Church. Nevertheless, it is both necessary and desirable to return at leisure, as often as time permits, in order to absorb the greatness and the full meaning of this ancient site.

Return then: best of all, at night, when all is quiet and the multitudes of the curious, the believers, the sceptical, and those who look for instant faith, have gone. All through the day, the monks and priests attend their duties and their offices, moving unruffled through the crowds who watch and pass amongst them. Then in the silent, watchful hours of night the Church reclaims her own, and this great house of God reveals the power of prayer generated through all the centuries long past. Responses echo back and forth, and immemorial chants rise up amid the smoke and incense. Stentorian voices ring through vaulted space, and twist and turn their way from distant chapels. The rise and fall of chanted prayers, gospels, invocations and creeds all take their turn with planned precision, wheeling like stars about the axis of the universe. Some voices come with confidence, treading a well-worn path to reaffirm that which is familiar. Others, more softly, seek and quest, for even now the truth is yet too large to comprehend. Lost in the bright enclosure of the Tomb the chanting fades away to murmurs. Measured time slips by, until at last the celebrant comes forth in robed and mitred splendour. Jewelled and proud, true representative of All Might, Majesty, Dominion and Power, bearded Byzantium thunders out the wondrous words: "Krystos anesti": "Christ is risen"; " Kyrie eleison".

Before the empty tomb the "struggle for deathlessness" is won.

Mediaeval pilgrims' crosses, carved in the stonework of the Church.

The Chapel of the Invention of the Cross.

Postscript

Through aeons of time, man's quest continues. Prophets, mystics, priests and rabbis may point the ways to faith and we may choose to follow whom we will, or turn aside. None has exclusive knowledge, nor, in our small corner of definable space, dare we assume exclusive rights. We can but seek a faith within ourselves, and give thanks to those who have gone before, leaving us earthly clues and indications for our aid.

And what of Jerusalem? The Holy City is still hedged about by war; still the inspiration and the cause of joy and suffering; still the challenge as of old; still waiting for the promise of a prophecy as yet unfulfilled, of peace for all who dwell within her walls. For Christian, Muslim and Jew, the mellow stone of Kalandia, and, for a deluded few, even the new frenetic skyline of the modern city, offer some representation and reflection of the other Jerusalem, that "heavenly city of the spirit": a heritage, surely, of such profound significance that were man to ignore it he would do so at his gravest peril.

. . . and you shall be my witness in Jerusalem . . .
and to the end of the earth.

Acts I:8

Eastern Orthodox archbishop and acolytes celebrate before the Tomb of Christ.

Entrance to the empty Tomb.

List of full-page illustrations

Pectoral cross of Lorraine of the Crusader period.

Jerusalem, seen from Mount Scopus, before the city was surmounted and enclosed by modern high-rise buildings after 1967.

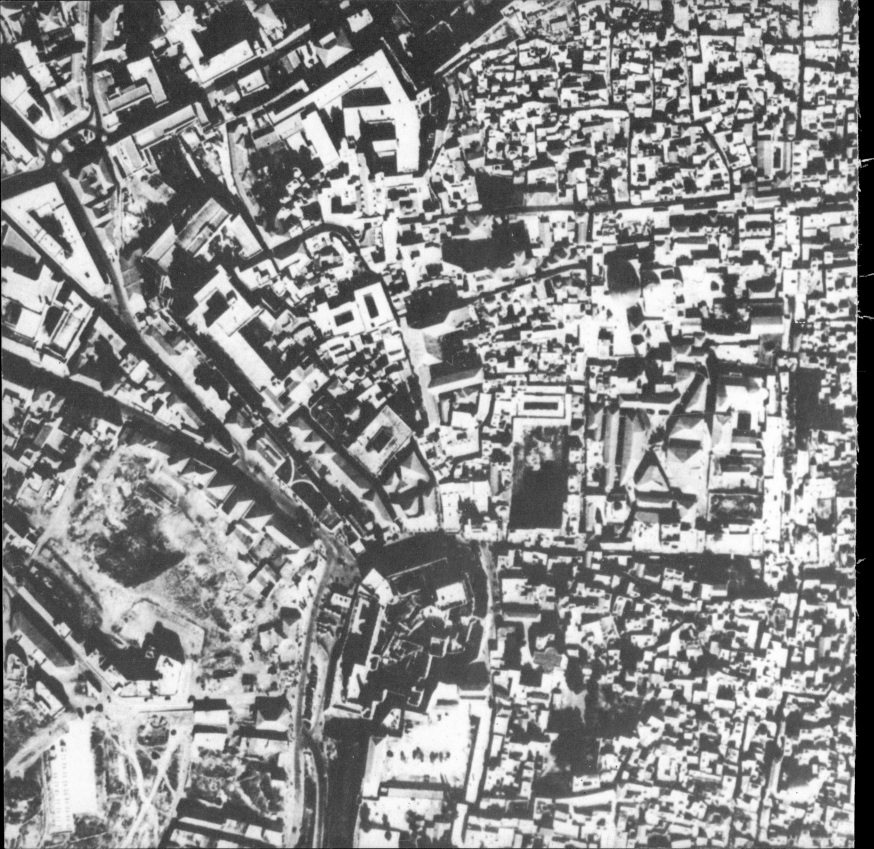